Dedication

Howz mom 'n'm?

Thank you, Gary Burbank, for giving radio voice these past twenty years to my wackiest thoughts. I am honored and thrilled on those occasions when I can make you laugh, sir—because you have made me laugh so much harder.

And given that *The Gary Burbank Show* is a community, I'm honored to also bow graciously to Burbank writers who have become more than challenging colleagues, but also fast friends, in alphabetical order ranked according to their smell: John Bunyan, Tim Mizak, Jim Probasco, Mary Tom Watts, Kevin Wolfe.

I must be off.

Acknowledgments

My gratitude to

- Jack Heffron for his first recognition of this book's possibilities
- Annie Sisson for not questioning why her husband kept chortling fervently at the keyboard at odd hours of the night
- Sandra Bond for laughing at mostly the right times (at the book, anyway) and subsequently selling the book anyway
- Dennis Chaptman for friendship and for challenging me to surrealistic humor extremes with his own surrealism
- Shakespeare for spelling it *theater* and to me for getting out of the theater biz just in time
- *Mad* magazine and, independently, Jay Ward of *Rocky and Bullwinkle* fame, for perhaps shaping my preadolescent sense of humor too damn much, as well as Richard Armour (and mostly Richard Armour) and the style of written humor that tickled and propelled me at an impressionable age (who else could demonstrate that footnotes could be rollickingly funny?)
- And, oh yeah, to *Green Acres*. I suspect I may be the first to thank *Green Acres* in a book's front matter, but as far as humor goes, *Green Acres* is the place to be.

Introduction

"The English language is nobody's special property. It is the property of the imagination: it is the property of the language itself."

—*Derek Walcott*

Never trust a bookstore employee who, when asked where to find etymology and word books, leads you to the word-search puzzle rack.

In the true story that prompted this advice, I stared at the pulp-paper acrostics and cryptograms and crosswords. Though a bit flummoxed, I realized that I should forgive this earnest associate. After all, English itself is, in a broad sense, a word puzzle, and like both those puzzles and the queries of where the etymology section of the bookstore is, sometimes people try hard yet come up with wrong answers. Our understanding of English—its history, its rules, its use—is often misconceived, misguided, misinformed, or based on some lie someone told us, probably via email, cuz it made a good story.

Yet, what a wondrous language. Puzzle me this language always, despite its inherent confounderies.

Yes, English is Swiss¹-cheesed with pitfalls, almost all of our own fermenting. Yes, there are 512.6 ways to pronounce the letter

---

¹ Oddly appropriate since the Swiss don't have a language of their own.

combination *o-u-g-h* from *through* to *tough* to *cough* to *plough* to
flough to *Brohough* (a branch of my family). Yes, English is known
kto khave kmore kpotential ksilent kletters kthan kactual kones.
Yes, we confuse our own spelling by respecting the languages we
borrow from to the point of retaining both original spelling and
pronunciation[2] (for example, we spell *rendezvous* and say *ron-day-
voo* but we don't write *rondayvu* or say *wren-dees-vows*). Yes, the
whole language is, in modern terms, a "mash-up" that allows slang
words like *mash-up* and *slang* to not only enter the language but also
become living, vibrant vocabulary. Yes, English is distended with
exceptions, oddities, antiquities, fossils, distractions, oxymorons,
shifts, speed bumps, flipflops, flummeries, and words with there
homonym[3] disasters. And, yes yes yes, everything you know about
English is wrong because of all the above.

Yet, all these negative *yes*es reflecting the influences, the exceptions, the what-the-hells-do-those-words-mean (not to mention the
fact that I can create odd plural words like "what-the-hells-do-those-
words-mean")—all these negative *yes*es bring to our language a flexibility, a luxuriant breeding ground for poetry, the foundation of
spelling bees, and (most important to this book) a dizzyingly high
platform for argument both fun and intense.

Everything You Know About English Is Wrong makes no attempt to
settle the arguments, and, in fact, (warning, verb use of *advocate*
lurking) I devil's-advocate occasionally purely to spur arguments. On
these pages, I regularly cross the line between descriptivism ("Hey,
grammar is as grammar does") and prescriptivism ("Conjugate properly or I'll rap your knuckles with a ruler, child!"). I take flexibly inflex-
ible stands on issues; point to little-known facts; force uptight word
watchers (those I've termed "the persnickitors") to tighten up even

---

[2] U.S. cities excepted, including Vye-enna (Vienna), Georgia; Ver-sayles (Versailles), Indiana;
Lye-ma (Lima), Ohio; Kay-ro (Cairo), Syrup—I mean, Illinois; and Mos-ko (Moscow—oops,
we changed that one to *not* reflect how English speakers would pronounce Moss-cow), Idaho.
[3] It's a joke. Honest. So their!

further by forcing them to follow their own rules. I make up a couple of things; repeat a few thoughts; point out "incorrect" answers to the puzzle we speak daily (from misconceptions about word histories to specious grammatical edicts to confusions about meanings, spellings and quotations). I repeat a few thoughts; I throw out some earthy words (you've been warned); and I battle with the persnickitors, with your sensibilities, and even with myself. Hopefully in good fun (yes—*hopefully*).

Please, the fun. The fun and the insight. I like what Dr. Elisabeth Piedmont-Marton of the University of Texas at Austin told the BBC when asked about the overall topic of language disagreements: "When they have spent hours arguing over whether it is correct to say, 'It is I' or 'It is me,' you have to wonder if they shouldn't be exploring something else about their relationship."

A Note to Kind and Forbearing Readers

In *Everything You Know About English Is Wrong*, I twist the occasional word and torture a few others, absolutely with intent. Similarly, I romp through a few, shall we say, innovative sentence structures. (I can't blame this on Steve Martin and the words he puts in Harris Telemacher's mouth in Martin's comedy *L.A. Story* when I do so, but I'll take the opportunity to quote him anyway: "the interesting word usements I structure.")[4]

Kind and forebearing readers, please always assume that such twists, tortures, and romps are always intentional. If I make an actual mistake anywhere on these published pages, I will alert you to said mistake right on the spot.

Thank you.
Bill Brohaugh

---

[4] And, oh yeah—I use footnotes.

The English Delusionary

A brief glossary of words I created for this volume of delusion-busters, for my own amusement and your annoyance:

- **Anacronymizer.** A creator of anachronistic acronyms.
- **Babblisciousness.** Really babblascious babble.
- **Bullshitternet.** Nonsense you find on the Internet.
- **Catapostrophe.** Bad use of apostrophes.
- **Chitchatternet.** Blather you find on the Internet; not nearly as pejorative as *bullshitternet.*
- **Definitive.** A "definite" fact that's usually wrong.
- **Delusionary.** For a definition, consult "The English Delusionary" on page 1.
- **Donce Words.** These are "dunce words for the nonce"—words I have created for the purposes of smartassery in a particular entry. Words like *smartassery.*
- **Etymologia Mythica.** Yeah, that would be my guess, too.
- **Flabasciousness.** See babblisciousness.
- **Lyricritic.** A persnickitor who attacks song lyrics.
- **Microparse.** To analyze a word or sentence down to its atoms, while forgetting that unlike matter, words often have no such structure. For an example, see "Double Negatives," page 122.
- **Notymology.** A blend word: not(et)ymology.
- **Persnickitor.** A hypersensitive stickler grammarian, one who screeches about using *hopefully* (see page 117) and other poster children of "bad" use of language without considering the depth and function of English. If you're persnickety, you persnicket. You are, therefore, a persnickitor.

- **Specious Histories & Ignorant Twaddle.** The phrase refers to acronyms. For full explanation, see page 57.
- **Xtreme Etymological Stasis.** Abbreviated *XeS* and pronounced by no mere coincidence "excess" (by me, anyway). This is the "if you're going to play that game" rule. A quick and simplistic example explored in more detail later: If you insist that *kudo* is an abominable mangling of the singular word *kudos*, then you must similarly insist that *pea* (the tasty vegetable you shouldn't eat with a knife) is an unacceptable mangling of the now obsolete singular word *pease*.

Everything You Know About English Is Wrong: **The Tut-Tutting Lectures**

The English Deceptionary

We begin *Everything You Know About English Is Wrong* with some simple word histories that we know to be deceptively wrong, because they are—as we see quickly with our first entry—unintentionally but decidedly pure . . .

BULL

File under "Shit, Bull": "Bull!" is not necessarily a scatological epithet.

If you believe that *bull* is short for *bullshit*, you are in essence bullshitting yourself.

Just as you don't mutter "Horse!" as a shortening of the horse-excrement epithet, you aren't speaking of bovine droppings when you use the word *bull*. The origins of this meaning of *bull* aren't fully clear, but the word did not result from earthy shortening. Bull could be related to the verb "to bull," which descends from the old French *bouler*, "to deceive." In English, *bull* the verb meant "to deceive or cheat" by the mid-1500s, and "to boast vacuously" by the mid 1800s. By the early 1600s, *bull* the noun versus *bull* the verb meant something that couldn't be, something self-contradictory. And its sense of "nonsense, insincerities, or lies" has been around since by 1915. But though *bull* is now synonymous with *BS*, it is not the same word.

And I wouldn't horse you about that.

HISTORY

File under "Story, His or Hers?": History is not a compound of "his story." Maybe.

When the word *history* was first used (by the late 1300s), it could mean any kind of recounting—true or false. A history could be false, and still be a history. So let's take a look at the history, both true and false, of the word *history* (which I would like to call history-squared or meta-history, except for the fact that we are looking at the word and not the study).

We've all heard of *herstory*, a clever but perhaps overused play on word. The word in question is, of course *history*, regenderized for a feminist twist. Many if not most people who use *herstory* know that the *his* in *history* is *not* the complement of *hers*; they're simply employing the same sort of wordplay that has given us such frequent and less-serious constructions as *hersterectomy*, *himnia/hisnia*, *womenopause* and *womenstruation*, and *galnocologist*. On the other hand, others promote the folk etymology that *history* compounds *his* and *story* seriously, whether or not they actually believe it. I like what I spotted on a blog entry about the word: "It should be history . . . for reasons of historiography (or, if you will—though I hope you won't—herstoriography: but can anyone say herstoriography with a straight face?)."

The truth is that *history* traces back through Latin as *historia*, which was borrowed from the Greek word meaning "narrative, recounting, or something learned by inquiring."

So you can see that there's no maleness to the word, despite the masculine disguise of the syllable *his* . . . though let's be true to the word *history* by learning something else by inquiring. If we take an additional step back, we find that the Greek *historia* is derived from the word *histor,* which had such meanings as "knowledge," "learning," and . . . um . . ."wise man." So, the wise man told . . . *his story.*

BONFIRE
The eighteenth-century wordmaster was not always right.

Bonfire: "a fire made for some publick cause of triumph or cele-bration." So writes the estimable Dr. Samuel Johnson in 1755's *Dictionary of the English Language.* And because Johnson was writing about the English language, he of course (*bien sur!*) imposed some French origins into a genealogically consistent native English word: *bonfire. -Fire* means, well, "fire." *Bon-,* Dr. Johnson espouses, is *bon*—"good," in French.

Well, that's all well and *bon,* except that in this case *bon* is native English for "bone." Not "good-fire," but "bone-fire." Including live human bones. Joan of Arc and supportive bones died in a bonefire. It's this grisly origin of the word that leads some people to cling to Dr. Johnson's etymology. But that, as the editors of *The Merriam-Webster New Book of Word Histories* argue, doesn't make etymological sense. Marrying French and native English is rare, and French's *bon* had been borrowed into English as *boon* (e.g., "boon companion"), and not *bon.*

Despite Dr. Johnson's mistaken contention, *bonfire* is a bad word. No bons about it.

QUICKSILVER
File under "Silver, Quick (and Hi Ho!)": Think fast: quicksilver is not speedy.

In a sad irony of word histories, the word *quicksilver* seems to be on its deathbed, in danger of being totally displaced and buried by the synonymous word *mercury*.

Quicksilver/mercury is an unusual metal in that it exists in liquid form at room temperature (and it bulges in old thermometers at greater-than-room temperature). Oldsters like me remember playing with globules of quicksilver from broken thermometers as kids, watching the blobs race around plates that we tilted to urge the blobs on. We were fascinated as the globules broke up into smaller blobs and coalesced again when they rammed into each other like living unicellular creatures. (Given modern concerns about mercury poisoning, today's youngsters will likely never again experience such astonishing Mr. Wizard moments.)

The sadness in the death of *quicksilver* lies partially in losing the innate poetry of the word. *Mercury* is mildly interesting because of its mythological connections (Mercury the planet racing around the sun in low orbit was named after the speedy Roman god who now has been relegated to commercial flower delivery). Interesting, though bland compared with evocative and vital *quicksilver*. I'm happy to say that elements of this poetry will be retained though deeply hidden in *hydrargyrum*, quicksilver's technical name and the source for HG on the Periodical Table of the Elements. You've already spotted the Greek root *hydra-* in this technical name, which literally means "water silver."

Yet, the primary and excruciating irony of the death of *quicksilver* arises from the original meaning of *quick*. Yes, those globules zipped in speedy races as I tilted and rotated the plate holding them when I was a kid. But their quickness was etymologically deceiving. The original meaning of *quick* is not "fast" or "speedy." It is "alive, infused with life." Living things move faster than, say, corpses, rocks or clumps of iron (and silver)—and because of that, meanings of *quick* eventually evolved into our current senses of "speedy, responsive, rapid." A quick wit is not a speedy wit; it is a wit that is alive. When you chew your fingernails to the quick, you are stripping the dead nails away to reveal the living, bleeding underskin. There is no non sequitur in the slow descent into quicksand, as it is "living sand."

So it is no mistake that I earlier compared quicksilver globs to one-celled creatures, and that I called quicksilver "vital"—in the sense that *vital* ultimately means "critical to life itself."

Quicksilver is silver that lives. We're losing that word. Its use is dying. Worse yet, in ironies of meanings, it is dying quickly.

PLANTAR WART
Planter's makes peanuts, and not warts.

The viral warts that afflict the bottoms of one's feet have nothing to do with the commercial franchise that brings us suave cartoon spokes-legume Mr. Peanut, he of debonair top hat, monocle, and cane. Granted, the agricultural nature of both the commercial Planter's name and the planting process that brings peanuts to market would link the product to barefoot planters who . . .

Well, my editor just slapped me before I slipped into some bullshitternet etymology. Anyone who has suffered those painful pedal "warts" has experienced plantar infections. *Pedal*, "of the foot," traces back to Latin, as does *plantar*, with the more specific meaning "of the sole of the foot." Even though *plantar* and the *plants* that planters plant while standing on their plantars trace back to the same Latin root (word root, not plant root), you do not suffer *planter's warts* (lucky you—they hurt, no matter the spelling); you suffer *plantar warts* (*ouch!*—believe me).

So if you have a have a painful plantar wart on your foot, go to a podiatrist. If you have a painful pedal wart on your foot, go to a plantariatrist. And if you have a painful planter's wart on your foot . . . likely you just stepped on a peanut—please be more careful when shelling those things, would you?

HONCHO

The feminine form of *honcho* is not *honcha,* and it's not *honchette,* either.

A few years back, an Internet blog entry carried this headline: "Homeland security honcha has phony PhD." The pedigree of the headline is pretty phony, too—etymologically speaking. The fact is that women can be honchos as easily as men can.

The conversion of the Spanish word *honcho* into the feminine-inflected *honcha* would be linguistically learned . . . if *honcho* were a Spanish word to begin with. It's Japanese: *han-cho,* meaning "squadron leader." So what are you really calling a female leader if you designate her as a honcha? On the subject, posted at about the same time as our unpedigreed headline, another blogger, going by the name Big Box of Paints, wrote: "honcha in Japanese is most likely to be read as . . . meaning a pure variety of Japanese green tea."

Ah. The so-called honcha is incorrectly acidic—with a phony Ph-tea.

SKOSH, TEMPURA
Tempura is not made with lutefisk.

The thought of sipping a bit of *sake*—just a skosh—with my tempura tickles me. Not the thought of the *sake*, for the moment, anyway (far be it from me to deny enjoying that warm rice wine, and I look forward to my next splash or two). What instead tickles me is using *skosh* and *tempura* in the same sentence, a real East/West fusion, that. *Tempura* is from the East . . . well, if you start in Japan and keep heading eastward across the Pacific, the Americas, and the Atlantic to Portugal. And *skosh* is from the West, if you retrace your steps westward all the way back to Japan.

Portuguese missionaries came to Japan in 1542, bringing with them Christianity, gunpowder, and a method of cooking fish by deep-frying it (not using gunpowder, mind you). The *Oxford English Dictionary* notes that *tempura* is probably adapted from Portuguese *tempero,* meaning "seasoning, flavoring, sauce, condiment," though it's also been suggested that it's related to *temporal,* "for a short time." Temporary? A short time? The thought's intriguing, because tempura is cooked quickly—for a short time—and was perhaps cooked by the missionaries during *temporary* periods without meat.

Now, if you haven't caught on that the Scandinavian-sounding *skosh* is ultimately of *Japanese* origin (despite the seeming Norsk monopoly on words with *S* and *K* in them), you've had a skosh too much *sake.* Or, more specifically, a sukoshi ("few") too much sake, slurring the word *sukoshi* into *skosh*—which is maybe how the word was slangishly borrowed back in the 1950s by English-speaking soldiers. Interestingly, the *U* is not voiced in the original version—

an unneeded letter contradictorily appearing in a word meaning "few."[5]

But back to the *sake*. I say, drink up! A skosh more! And *skoal!* (But drive responsibly between Japan and Portugal . . .)

A.D./B.C.
In one year and out the other.

There are many things that the abbreviation pair A.D./B.C. is not. A.D./B.C. is not a classic heavy metal band, not a proposed reordering of the first four letters of the alphabet, and not short for "After Death/Before Christ"—at least not the first part.

The years B.C. did indeed take place before the birth of Christ (as did about five years A.D., as historians have determined that Christ was probably actually born in 6 A.D.). And *B.C.* indeed stands for "before Christ." However, the common misconception that A.D. stands for "After Death" results from applying the convention of its partner in time—non-Latin wording—to an ultimately Latin abbreviation.

First, consider the logic of a supposed "After Death" abbreviation: designating the year of Christ's birth as the year 1 After Death would hint that Jesus got a whole lot accomplished in a pretty darn short time. *A.D.* is actually Latin: *Anno Domini*, "The Year of Our Lord."

And as long as we're casting about with *C* abbreviations, I will make brief mention of the PC crowd—the politically correct crowd. There's movement to replace B.C./A.D. with B.C.E./C.E., abbreviating "Before the Common Era/Common Era" in an effort to remove specific Christian reference. This is misguided from a linguistic standpoint. Keep in mind that I've been using this space to tell you

---

[5] Because *sukoshi* means "few," perhaps there's room for a Sake Lite—see "Light/Lite, Night/Nite" on page 156 to see what that's all about.

that *Everything You Know About A.D. Is Wrong,* because folk etymology has led people to misinterpret the abbreviation. To the PC crowd, I say, go ahead—substitute another abbreviation, which will in turn be misinterpreted, likely using the very *C* word you're trying to replace. In fact, I contend that *B.C.E.* will be commonly misinterpreted as "Before the Christian Era," and *C.E.* as the "Christian Era" by previous association with the phrase "Before Christ"—a designation used for many centuries A.D. and/or C.E. now. That reference is far better hidden in the not-so-easily interpretable *A.D.* Thus, you will accomplish the precise opposite of the PC goal.

And all that means extra work for me. Likely I'll have to update future editions of this book to explain that *C.E.* stands for "Common Era" and not "Christian Era," in an essay I'll likely title "PCE: In the Year of the Common Error."

FEMALE
Female is related to *male* only by marriage.

The word *female* is a diminutive, the way that *novelette* is a diminutive of *novel*—it is a shorter novel. *Female* is not a diminutive of *male,* even though females are usually shorter than males, which is a sad joke and I apologize. *Female* ultimately comes from a diminutive of the Latin word *femina*—in Latin, *femella* meant "little woman," and it came to English through French as *femelle.*

So female readers don't feel slighted, the word *male* also comes from a Latin source—*mas*—and the diminutive *masculus,* meaning "little man," which eventually came to us through Old French as *male.*

Because the concept of *femelle* is so closely related to that of *male* (related but opposite, as you may have noticed), we began altering the spelling of *femelle* to coincide with the spelling of *male*. Not surprising, actually. Just more proof that opposites attract.

OUTRAGE

There is no rage in *outrage*.

If you were to tell me that I was outside the norm, beyond moderation, extravagant, and strangely dressed, *I would be outraged!*

And I'd probably agree with you. But even if I didn't agree, I wouldn't necessarily be angry about your claim.

You see, when the word *outrage* and its derivatives came to us in Middle English from Old French, it had nothing to do with rage at all. So you can see what I mean, let's split the word into two syllables.

Out-rage. Right?

Wrong—at least when the word started out. Let's return one of the original letters to the word and try that split again: *outre-age.*

Outré is an Old French word meaning "beyond." And the state of beyondness was *outre-age,* somewhat along the lines of the state of draining being *drainage,* the state of assembling being *assemblage,* and the state of messing being *message* (well, I made that last one up).

The original *outrage,* before we borrowed it into English around the 1300s, was something "beyond" propriety—an insult or some other transgression. When we brought it into English, *outrage* had intensified beyond (or outré) mere impropriety to insolence or even violence. To be outraged in the early 1700s was to be violated; by the 1800s, to be appalled or, in a common modern sense, to be infuriated, enraged.

By the way, a side note: *outrageous* is outrageously verbose. If something is outrageous in the modern sense of the word, it is also—simply and sleekly—*outré*.

THREE SHEETS TO THE WIND

I was not drunk when I wrote this entry. Well, maybe I was. I can't remember.

For a long time, I puzzled over the euphemistic phrase "three sheets to the wind," meaning "drunk." I understood "blitzed." The term "shitfaced" is a little oblique, but not in any way beyond immediate comprehension. "Blotto" I got. "Trashed," "hammered," "nicely irrigated with horizontal lubricant," "zombied," "wasted," "pissed up" (for the Brits)—all these things I understood. But unless the sheets had something to do with college-debauched toga parties or the comfy coverings under which I would pass out, I wasn't quite catching on.

Something to do with sailboats, I remembered, when teetering to a vaguely upright position the next morning, and indeed the cliché exhibits nautical origin in rare defiance of the wordorigins.org CANOE theory, which forecasts the tendency to assign sea-going origins to words (for more on this, see also a delicately unnamed entry beginning on page 58). I was still puzzled, figuring that a sailboat with three billowy sails being pressed ahead by steady winds would sail smoothly and powerfully, without crossing the centerline once, twice, *ohmygawd!*, flashing lights in my rearview mirror! Sheet, man!

The phrase "three sheets to the wind" implied to me "full sail." But, because I've done very little sailing, sober or otherwise, I had no clue that the sheets are not the bedsheet-like sails that puff up proudly in the wind—the sheets are the ropes that hold the sails in place. Four sheets, four ropes, per sail. *Sheet* in this sense traces back to Old English, as does the fabric-version of the word, but with different origins.

Now, if a couple of those ropes lose their mooring to the boat, the wind will whip both the sheets and the sail about vigorously. If three of the four sheets on a sail are loose, the ship will likely move erratically, slur its words, cross the centerline once, twice, *ohmygawd!*, flashing lights in my rearview mirror!

RESOUND
Resound does not sound like it looks like.

Last night I heard a sports announcer say something that sounded a bit strange. And then sounded a bit strange again—in essence, it re-sounded. "The ninth-inning comeback against the Cincinnati Reds made a re-sounding statement!" Yes, *re-sound,* with a pronounced *S* instead of a pronounced *Z* in the middle.

A statement that (zounds!) resounds does indeed re-sound—it echoes. The *sound* in *resound* is the sound that you would expect. So where does the *reezound* pronunciation come in? Ultimately, the word comes from Old French and retains its imported pronunciation. Interestingly, when the word was brought into English around the late 1300s, it was spelled *resoun,* but the spelling eventually changed in analogy of the word *sound.* So we changed the spelling to conform to the word *sound,* but we didn't change the pronunciation to conform to the word *sound.* Therefore, to properly pronounce *resound,* think of the pronunciation of its close relative, *resonate.*

Ah, *resonate*. Let's see if our friend the sports announcer can re-sound that one. Perhaps to rhyme with *Cincinnati?*

PEN, PENCIL, PENIS, PEST, PESTER (IN ALPHABETICAL ORDER)
None of the above words are related. Although I could be lying.

Late twentieth-century satire magazine *Spy* used to run a hilarious feature called "Separated at Birth?," in which the editors juxtaposed the photos of two absolutely unrelated (we think) celebs, public figures and notorious sorts who looked remarkably alike. Two of my favorite installments were Yasser Arafat paired with Ringo Starr, and on the even more obscure side, Muammar Kaddafi paired with game-show ubiquitor Bert Convy (who had no identifiable credential for being on game shows other than the fact that he was always on game shows).

Let's play that game a bit, with some Starrs and Arafats (Kaddafis and Convys are too passé). *Separated at birth?* Guess which two of the following three pairs team unrelated parentage, and which one indeed represents direct bloodlines:

• *pest/pester*
• *pen/pencil*
• *pencil/penis* (sorry, I couldn't resist)

Did you spot the two unrelated pairs? And the pair of words that *are* related?

Let's take up the unrelated ones first—starting with the pair whose non sequitarianism is perhaps most difficult to discern: *Pester* did not originally mean "being a pest." *To pester* was "to impede," and is likely related to an obsolete English verb *impester,* meaning "hobble," which probably traces back through French to an assumed Latin word (*impastoriare*) meaning "hobble." The past of *pest* is a bit more severe. When it came into English, it was used to mean the Black Death—the bubonic plague. *Pest* traces through French back to *pestis*, the Latin word for "pestilence."

Then there's option #3, for which I apologize: *pencil/penis*. Yes, they look alike, and as I said, I couldn't resist . . . because they *are* the related words. *Penis* is Latin for "tail" or, um, "penis" (likely by vulgar Latin slang use of the "tail" meaning). *Pencil* came to us a figurative use of the diminutive of *penis*—"little tail"—meaning "brush." In English, a pencil was a brush before it was a writing instrument.

And that convenient red herring *pen/pencil*? *Pen* does so very much look like a shortening of *pencil*, but the word for the writing tool comes from French *penne*—"feather," as in a feather quill.

A little advice: If you're writing this all down . . . use a pen.[6]

JOURNEYMAN
A journey of a thousand miles begins with a single day.

A journeyman has nothing to do with travel, as the word *journey* would imply. But then again, originally the word *journey* had no exclusive connection with travel.

We borrowed *journey* from an Old French word with various meanings of "a day" or "things accomplished in a day" (things like work performed, travels recorded, and so on). In English, an early and now-obsolete meaning of *jurneis* or *iourneye* or many other spellings was "day," with the meaning of travel following

---

[6] For more on "Separated at Birth?" words, see "*Isle/Island*" on page 131.

shortly because of the word's connection with its Old French source.

But at first, a journeyman was a day-worker, thus the word's current meaning of one skilled, but only to a point. And so, I shall *adjourn* this discussion (put off to another day), so that you may write this factoid down in your daily record. No, not your blog. Your *journal*.

GARDENIA
The plural of *gardenium* is not *gardenia*.

Though a gardenia grows from a garden, the word *gardenia* did not grow from the word *garden*—not the generic word, anyway. If I were a bullshitternet "Did You Know!!!!?" guy, I'd explain that the floral name *gardenia* comes from the Latin word *gardenium* ("domesticated plant"), and was actually originally a plural. But it wasn't. There's no such word as *gardenium*.

Granted, a smidgeon (or two smidgeia) of Latin exists in the name of the plant—in the sense that *gardenia* puts into a Latin "form" the last name of one coincidentally named Alex Garden, an American naturalist, who was honored by having the plant named after him in 1760. And for all you etymology hoaxers out there, just as prostitutes did not take one of their slang names from a general named Hooker (see page 86), flower and vegetable truck farms did not take their name from Mr. Garden. The word *garden* was not home-grown; it came to us in the 1300s from Old North French.

Because of its horticultural roots, I wonder why it wasn't restricted by customs.

MINUSCULE
There is no *mini* in *minuscule.*

If you spell one word meaning "very small" as *miniscule,* hold on for a minute.

And by *minute,* I don't mean the noun designating a bit of time and pronounced *minnit.* I mean the adjective meaning "very small" and pronounced *my-noot.* (Actually, in a sense, I mean them both, because ultimately they're the same word.)

The first word in question is spelled *minuscule,* and the key syllable is *minus-* and not *mini-,* even though the latter seems to make sense by analogy with *miniature, mini-van, mini-mouse,* etc. *Minus,* of course, is "minor, lesser," and *-cule* is a diminutive of that, making the lesser even less. (A "mini-scule" would be a tiny campus in Scotland, as *scule* is one recorded Scot spelling of *school.*) The ultimate source of *minuscule* is, of course, Latin, though we borrowed it from French. The earliest meaning of *minuscule* in English was its French meaning, the example of which has already appeared in this entry dozens of times. A minuscule is a lower-case letter, and the word eventually was extended to other things small.

Ultimately, though, you are safe to remember this spelling-bee guideline: to spell *minuscule* correctly, remember to "Hold on for a minute."

THROWS AND THROES
Don't let the distinction between the two words throe you.

Two often-confused words are *throw* (with a bunch of meanings, from "the act of throwing" to a type of shawl) and *throe* (primarily with meanings of sudden movement, jerking, convulsion—either physical or mental). So, one way to alarm the persnickitors is to write something like "George was in the throws of passion . . ."

Now, maybe George was actually getting entangled with a paramour wearing a pretty sexy shawl, but that's unlikely given that not many shawls are sexy and that by the time you hit the stage of passionate throes, usually the shawls and other accoutrements have been dispensed with. So, literate writers are careful to distinguish between, say, the throws that hit a baseball batter in the ribs, and the throes of anger that will likely result.[7]

Except . . .

If you want to start an argument with a persnickitor, you could point out that earlier spellings of *throe* include *throwe* and—as recorded as late as 1773—*throw*.

CHILE/CHILI/CHILLY

Chile is not chilly, chili is not chilly, and never the twain shall meet.

Chili peppers hot,
Chile peppers cold,
Chilly peppers in the pot, nine centuries old.

This, of course, is a recast of the old "pease porridge" nursery rhyme, infused with a different set of concepts to make a point about the verbal porridge representing the relationship between chili peppers, the country of Chile, and the chilly reception you'll get from etymologists if you suggest that any of these words are connected.

CHILI PEPPERS HOT: *Chili* (the pepper and ultimately the stew made with the pepper) traces back through Spanish to the native

---

[7] Here of course we're talking about careful writers. Speakers are free to say "The throws of" whatever anytime they want; I suspect no one would notice.

South American Nahuatl word for the pepper plant. It is not, as Dutch physician and botanist Jacobus Bontius wrote in 1631, a "quasi dicas Piper e Chile" ("named as if a pepper from Chile," if my Latin translation is anywhere in the same hemisphere as the actual meaning, but then again, remember that I tried to translate "E Pluribus Unum" by myself as a kid, and could only come up with "made of lead").

CHILE PEPPERS COLD: One might say that the etymological trail to *Chile* has grown cold. Though we're not sure how the country name originated, no possibilities connect it with the hot pepper plant, and one possibility even suggests that it comes from native *tchili*, meaning "snow," from the native South American language Aymara, or a word from the native South American language Quecha: *chili* meaning "cold" or "snow" or, yes, "chilly." But even so:

CHILLY PEPPERS IN THE POT, NINE CENTURIES OLD: Our adjective *chilly* and its source noun *chill*, meaning "cold," traces all the way back to Old English. And just to confuse matters, one early spelling of *chill* was *chile*.

Why do I spend so much time disassociating *chili* and *Chile* and *chilly*? Well, I hail from the Cincinnati area, where a favorite local dish is a bed of spaghetti, topped with a spiced meat sauce (cinnamon among the spices), chopped onions, beans and grated cheese. This dish is Cincinnati chili, and it, too, has nothing to do with any of the aforementioned chilis. And yes, you Texans and Mexicans and Chileans, we know it's not "real" chili, and, by gosh, we don't care.

PEANUT
Peanuts are not nuts.

The *nut* in *peanut* is misleading. Peanuts are legumes. Other legumes are beans, lentils, and alfalfa—the latter of which I point out not to give you a third example, but just because *alfalfa* is a cool word I don't get to use too often.

And now that we're throwing odd botanical terms about, let's shell a few more "nuts":

Coconuts are drupes (I'm scared to look up that word).[8] Brazil nuts are seeds. Macadamia nuts are follicles (not the kind you grow your eyebrows with, and a good thing, too). Between Brazil nuts and macadamia nuts, at least Brazil nuts are partially truthful. They originate in Brazil. Macadamia nuts do *not* originate in Macadamia. (Did I shatter your illusions?) They originated in Scotland![9] Well, the nuts actually originated in Australia, as Macadamia is not a country. The *name* originated in Scotland, because the botanical name *macadamia* comes from a Scottish chemist named John Macadam.

Now, on the other hand, peanuts *are* nuts. The other peanuts. Dwarf chestnuts. The *Oxford English Dictionary* declares that the use of *pea nuts* to describe dwarf chestnuts is rare and now obsolete, but the first recorded reference to *pea nuts* (1794) predates the now-familiar use of the term by almost a decade.

That's perhaps too much history and science to explain that you're nuts if you think nuts are nuts. So let's wander back to peanuts, at least the ones we don't have roasting over an open fire

---

[8] But my editor made me do it anyway. To oversimplify botanically, a fruit with a pit is a drupe—like a plum or an olive. Now I feel better.

[9] Hint: Use of exclamation points usually indicates "this etymology is full of it," thus their extensive use in bullshitternet revelations.

at Christmastime in that one song but evidently nowhere else. There are a number of reasons that we mislabel these legumes as nuts, but I prefer my explanation. What baseball vendor in his right mind is going to go through the stands yelling "Legumes! Get your salted legoooooomes!"?

CURMUDGEON

File under "Johnson, Samuel": I find myself once again disagreeing with the eighteenth-century wordmaster with curmudgeonly respect.

I'm a curmudgeon. You know, cranky, grouchy, skeptical, stubborn. And only curmudgeons would have the audacity to grouse at the esteemed Dr. Samuel Johnson, compiler of 1755's *Dictionary of the English Language*, a momentous and trailblazing work to which English-watchers (and -speakers) owe incredible debt. But, because I am a curmudgeon, I must point out that Dr. Johnson's dictionary told us that the word *curmudgeon* "is a vitious manner of pronouncing coeur mechant"—a phrase using two French words that can be regarded as meaning "heart of evil." OK, it fits, but it's wrong. No one knows exactly where the word came from. Some people believe that the word came from a word meaning "hoarder of grain," a nasty grain thief. The source of this fanciful explanation (with the background that *corn* once meant grain in general) was a 1600 translation of Livy's *History of Rome* by Philemon Holland. The Latin word *frumentarius*, meaning "corn dealer," was translated (in a play on words so arcane that it took etymologists about 300 literal years to "get it") as the *cornmudgin*.

Now, the grain-fed etymology is wrong, too. I know that. But, as a curmudgeon with an odd sense of humor making jokes that take people years to "get," I find it exceedingly difficult to definitively dispute the *"corn* dealer" explanation . . . [10]

TEETOTALER
File under "Total, T": Teetotalers do not specifically drink tea.

The etymology of *teetotaler* causes some folk etymologists trouble, which starts with *T* which rhymes with *P* which stands for *pool!*

That of course is an homage to *The Music Man,* the Meredith Wilson musical in which con man Harold Hill arrives in River City, Iowa, to bilk the locals. His scam: after convincing parents that kids need a wholesome pursuit (like forming a marching band[11]) to draw them away from temptation, he'd take preorders on musical equipment, intending to abscond with their cash.

In his con pitch, Harold Hill mostly warns against playing pool, which starts with *P* and rhymes with *T,* which stands for *trouble,* but he also invokes the treachery of drink, including "beer from a bottle" escalated from the seemingly innocent beginnings of sipping "medicinal wine from a teaspoon," which starts with *T* which rhymes with *tea,* which doesn't stand for *teetotaler.*

In this little musical lesson you can see the "trouble" some people in River City have with the origins of the word *teetotaler.* A common misspelling of *teatotaler* reflects the logical but incorrect assumption that abstainers from drink turn to tea. We're not sure exactly how the word formed, but wordwatchers agree that

---

[10] If any of my jokes in this book seem completely opaque, check back with me in 300 years—it may take me that long to clarify a few things.

[11] Engaging in wholesome bake sales would have made for a somewhat more pedestrian musical. "76 pound cakes in the big parade!"

the *tee* in *teetotaler* is the letter *T.* It may be short for *temperance,* or even for *total.* It may be an intensifier, kind of a short way of saying *"total with a capital T!"* Which rhymes with *C,* which stands for *creator,* and the creator of the word *teetotaler* has been said to be one Dicky Turner who was buried in Preston, England, in 1847. In fact, this claim to authorship appears on Turner's Preston tombstone. Even though Turner's "creation" is generally debunked, I want to believe it, not for any etymological or even logical reasons, but as a vote from the heart. I've been placing the etymological rhyming words into the mouth of Harold Hill, the *Music con-Man,* because in interesting coincidence, Harold was first and most famously played by the dynamic, powerful singer/actor, Robert *Preston.*

DIALOGUE
A dialogue does not have seating limits.

The following is pure myth, and Greek myth at that: "Only two people can engage in dialogue."

Any number of people can engage in dialogue, for two reasons. One is that other than *monologue,* we have no accepted words specifying the number of people in conversation—for instance, we have but rare use of *trialogue,* no *quatralogue,* no *sesquilogue,* no *kilologue* (even in these social networking days).

The other, more important, reason is that the *di-* in *dialogue* has nothing to do with the number *two,* not even back through the word's Latin and Greek origins. *Dialogue* traces back to Greek *dialegsthai,* "to converse." *Dialegsthai* is also the ultimate source of another of our language words: *dialect.* So, let's for a moment employ the persnickitorial logic of the law of Xtreme Etymological Stasis (the "two people can play *that* game" rule): if only two people can engage in dialogue, then there can be only two dialects.

And that is the end of *this* monologic *di*atribe.

TRIAGE

The word *triage* does not have three etymologies.

Etymologies can be triaged into three distinct categories:

    1) *True etymologies*
    2) *Deceiving etymologies*
    3) *False etymologies*

They can also be triaged into a fourth category:

    4) *Etymologies that have nothing to do with the concept of three*

And we shall triage the word *triage* into that fourth category.

Some of you are wondering how a word so clearly based on the Latin/Greek prefix *tri-* can be used in the context of organizing into any number of categories. And the answer is that historically *triage* has nothing to do with the concept of *three,* thus its inclusion in category 4 (and its applicability to category 2). The *tri-* is related to *try,* a verb that has various meanings of selection, testing, culling.

Triage, the French noun indicating the action of the verb *trier* ("to cull"), came to us by the early 1700s. *Trier* is the source of our verb *to try,* from a much earlier borrowing, from Old French. Try a new restaurant—investigate it. Try a defendant—in essence, cull out the truth. Try your patience—test it. (And lord knows I've tried. . . .)

Triage denoting *three* has been bolstered by war-time medical triage (from World War I), in which the wounded were prioritized—coincidentally into three groups—according to those who needed immediate attention, those who could survive a wait while more serious injuries were attended to, and those who were unlikely to survive at all. Yet, these three distinctions are not upheld in the medical world these days. Here's a note I spotted on the website of the Australian Institute of Health and Welfare: "Patients will be triaged into one of five categories on the National Triage Scale according to the triageur's response to the question: 'This patient should wait for medical care no longer than . . . ?'" Perhaps they should call this *quintrage* instead of triage, and if so, we'd have to triage the history of *quintrage* into a fifth category:

    5) *Smart-aleck etymologies*

Reredundancy Rerevisited

In a section of this book called "Reredundancy Rerevisited" on pages 29, 29 and 29, I . . .

But I repeat myself. Just read on to learn that many redundancies aren't really, and that some redundancies are actually not only less annoying than this introduction, but also actually good for you.

HOI POLLOI

File under "Polloi, Hoi": There is no English redundancy in the phrase, "the hoi polloi."

One of my favorite quotes about writing comes from Bil Gilbert, the late *Sports Illustrated* columnist, who warned writers: "Writing is not glamorous. It is not appearing on *The Tonight Show*. It is my job. It is sitting in the damn basement, worrying about the word *the*."

Note that Bil was *not* worried about the word *hoi*.

I seem to read the argument about the phrase *hoi polloi* more than I read or hear the words in actual use. The persnickitors point out—and correctly so, I fully acknowledge—that literally translated from Greek, *hoi polloi* means "the many." So if I speak of "the hoi polloi," I am actually uttering words meaning "the the many."

All well and good, but I argue against this particularly technicality for several reasons.

Let's begin not with grammar but with the sound of the language. The sentence "The choice was popular with hoi polloi," sounds, to my ear, lacking. If you understand the term, the sentence begs for an English "the." If you don't understand the term, and I'd wager that more don't than do (there's a reason "It's all Greek to me" continues to live—for that reason see page 103), the sentence seems to sound as if the choice was popular with someone named Hoi Polloi. (Compare "The choice was popular with baker" and "The choice was popular with the baker.")

Next, we already assimilate the word *the* as expressed in various languages into words we use every day. ("The al-Qaeda base"—"the the base base.") Or, for that matter, several other Arabic borrowings (the "meanings" in parentheses in the following examples represent present spellings, not source spellings): including "the essence" (*al-cohol*), "the calcined ashes" (*al-kali*), "the sea eagle" (*albatross*), and "the early blooming fruit" (*al-pricot*). Or moving to Spanish, how about "The Las Vegas plain," which literally means "the the fertile plain plain"; "the alligator," meaning "the the lizard"; or "the alpaca," meaning "the the llama." (I have to admit a certain affection for "the the" preceding the *el el* spelling of *llama*.) Let's let the French into it, too: "the ammunition," meaning "the the munition." And my favorite such "redundancy" involves the professional baseball team that began as The Los Angeles Angels. That name translates into "the the angels angels." (The team moved to Anaheim, calling themselves, of course, the Anaheim Angels, but then, without actually moving a single bat out of its rack, changed its name to the Anaheim Angels of Los Angeles, in essence, "the angels of the angels," kind of a different *créme de la créme*.) So why should the phrase *hoi polloi* have to wear the batross around its neck and not also be granted such assimilation?

Third, as I often point out in this book, we speak English and not [fill in the source language in question here]. And by the precepts of the law of Xtreme Etymological Stasis (XeS), if you're going to do unto *polloi* by insisting that *hoi* be properly interpreted, why don't we do unto others in the same way?: "My plane landed at Los Angeles airport," instead of "My plane landed at the Los Angeles airport." Better yet, perhaps we should XeS the sentence to read "My plane landed at Hoi Angeles airport."

Fourth, I find it interesting to note that the *Oxford English Dictionary* cites seven manuscripts using the phrase *hoi polloi* over the centuries. Five of the seven references insert English *"the"* before the phrase. Granted, two references were from learned authors, John Dryden and Lord George Gordon Byron, which would explain the two holdouts. Would, but doesn't. Both Dryden and Byron use that icky *the*-word before *hoi polloi*.

Fifth, I believe the persnickitors should concern themselves not with definite articles, but with indefinite meanings. *Hoi polloi* is in danger of losing its original meaning of the "the many, the masses" as it becomes associated with *hoity-toity*, a word with similar sounds and rhythms and a significantly contrary meaning. Although, I might find myself relishing the time when hoity-toity persnickitors have lost their grasp on the general meaning of *hoi polloi* because they were overly concerned about that rascally *the*. (And as an aside, I wonder if anyone has ever misinterpreted *hoity-toity* as "the tytoity." And such misinterpretation would give interesting new meaning to the Chinese condiment, hoisin, "the sin" sauce, which of course it is not.) The true irony of the shifting meaning of *hoi polloi* by association with *hoity-toity* is that *hoity-toity* has its roots in words basically meaning "rabble-rousing."

Finally, word use and acceptance is ultimately a matter of democracy (another Greek donation, that). So if the masses—hoi polloi with or without the *the*—want to say "the hoi polloi," then so be it.[12]

---

[12] Even though I hate footnotes to the point that I continually use them, I want to point out that when said aloud—which happens, um, all the time—*hoi polloi* sounds like an Australian greeting. "Hoy! Palloy!" Kind of like the down-under version of a Brooklyn "Hey, pally!"

SAHARA

With apologies to the musicals (see page 200): Sierra, Sahara—let's call the whole thing off.

Two points:

    1) The phrase "Sahara Desert" is redundant.

    2) I don't care.

To be technical, *Sahara* means "desert" in Arabic. So, saying "Sahara Desert" is literally saying "desert desert." Unlike the persnickitors, however, I don't fret about this "problem." And by the same token, I don't care if someone refers to "The Sierra Nevada Mountains," even though the phrase roughly means "The Mountains Snow-Clad Mountains" to those literate in Spanish. (Too bad there are no Sierra Montana Mountains—which would mean, roughly, "Mountains Mountains Mountains.")

Demanding that I not use English words that happen to duplicate the meaning of non-English words is, to me, like adhering to the guideline, "When in Rome, do as the Romanians do." (See my rant about *hoi polloi* on page 29 for specifics as to why.)

Specific to the Sahara, I grant you that I speak the occasional Arabic, as we all do when using such imported words as *alkali* (which finds its way into my daily conversations at least hourly) and *alcohol* (which finds its way into my daily conversations . . . well, back to the original subject . . .). I was even speaking Arabic in a sense in my opening to this entry, by using Arabic numerals. But other than that, I tend to speak little Arabic on a daily basis. So I ask that you forgive my occasional multilingual redundancy. It might be uneducated worldliness, but it is not uneducated *English*.

Now, despite all that, I'll now turn around and say that you should almost never have to say Sahara *Desert*. Even with the existence of other Saharas (the casino, primarily), people will know what you mean when you use just the *S*-word. I strongly recommend referring to just "the Sahara" as a matter of concision, of using what the reader/listener understands the word to communicate, rather than what it literally means in another language that you didn't happen to study in high school. This admonition springs from the same principle as not referring to "the city of Chicago" when readers/listeners understand through context, experience or both that Chicago is a city (and not because *Chicago* means "city," which it doesn't). After all, "Editing to maximize every word" is my middle name.[13]

My opinion of worrying about "Sahara Desert" for reasons of purity of meaning rather than of pure wordiness can be summarized by my delight in a subtle joke I found in a Monty-Pythonesque video game called *Dungeon Runners*. The focal location in the game, where all players go to get equipment and store their stuff, is a small community named "Townston"—which I hereby nominate as the capital city of The Sahara Desert Desert, located along the scenic Mountains Mountains Mountains.

ISLAND-ISLAND
No man is an ig.

Most of you know that phrase as "No man is an island." John Donne, of course, in *Devotions upon Emergent Occasions*, also the source of "therefore never send to know for whom the bell tolls; it tolls for thee." (And some other analogies you should be aware of: see the entry for "Donne, Un-Donne" on page 107 for more on this.)

---

[13] Literally. Honest. "Editing to maximize every word" is my legal middle name, although the foresightful and clever folks filling out my birth certificate truncated the phrase, with a slight respelling (Editing to maximize every weard), to *Edward*.

Donne's words continue, "No man is an island, entire of itself; every man is a piece of the continent, a part of the main. If a clod be washed away by the sea, Europe is the less, as well as if promontory were, as well as if a manor of thy friend's or of thine own were. Any man's death diminishes me . . ."

Donne was not wrong in his metaphor of human being as non-island, as by the time he published the above quote (1624), the word *island* fully meant a bit of land completely surrounded by water. What Donne may not have realized, and what few of us realize, is that in its etymological roots, the word *island* is self-redundant, and in these etymological roots, a man could be both an island *and* a piece of the continent.

Island was originally a compound word in Old English, spelled *igland*. *Ig* meant "island," and *land* meant, um, "land."

Island-land? It makes sense if you consider that an early meaning of *igland/iland/island* was "a body of land bordered by water, but not necessarily completely." (For more on this, including how that rascal *S* found its way into the word, see the entry for "Isle/Island" on page 131). And that's how someone could indeed be an island *and* a piece of the continent.

I believe I have now witnessed infinity. *Island* really means "island-land," which therefore really means "island-land-land," which therefore means "island-land-land-land," which therefore really means . . . which therefore really means it's time for me to shut up.

LUKEWARM

Luke did not come to the warm side.

Word watchers give tautological redundancies a lukewarm reception, as well they should. Such a reception represents a perfect marriage of form and content.

Or as well they shouldn't. Because, in a sense, to give a lukewarm reception would be to engage in tautology as bad as the repetitiously repetitive "tautological redundancies" above. The adjective *luke,* largely obsolete since the days of Middle English but still apparently in dialectical use, meant what the word *lukewarm* now denotes: "tepid." So, historically, our word *lukewarm* means lukewarmwarm.

So, word watchers, is use of *lukewarm* now heating you up a bit?

GOOD GOOD REDUNDANCY
Not all redundant phrases are bad.

As the author of a book called *Write Tight,* I've spent a good share of my time tut-tutting about redundant, clichéd, or just plain boring word pairs, like *fast and furious, pure and simple,* and *sick and tired.* On the other hand, there are a handful of common word pairs that I will admonish only gently. The couples in this group often contribute to wordiness, and I advise against their use, but I honor something the pairs are doing. They are watching out for each other; a strong word tends to its ailing mate, keeping it alive in the language, even while no other words give succor. For example, where would *vim* be without its friend *vigor,* in the phrase "vim and vigor." Where would *fro* be without *to, hue* without *cry, pomp* without *circumstance, wrack* without *ruin?* Nowhere. We'd be losing the fading weaker member of the team from the language completely. And *"hem and haw"*?—neither would still be about without the other.

In the case of "vim and vigor," I concede any number of reasons to avoid the phrase. It's a cliché, and an outdated-sounding one at that. It's largely redundant, as both words connote energy. Still, the youngster *vim* (from the 1800s) zipping about with its determined, experienced mentor *vigor* (from before Chaucer's time) demonstrates an energetic nuance that's a shame to lose.

Certain tired phrases carry the burden of suffering disdain so they might keep archaic and useful words alive in some form. Is the word *madding* ever used except in allusion to Thomas Hardy's *Far from the Madding Crowd*? Have you ever seen any kind of *shrift* except a short one? Is something that's as expected "in" *kilter*? Examples of fading words preserved in the museum cases of outdated phrasings are rife—and there's even a word for them, a word appropriate for museum cases: *fossil*. I respect the clichés for these acts of preservation even as I suggest that we avoid them. I mourn the loss of words like *vim* and *wrack* and *madding*, but I concede that we need to close up the museums at night and go about our daily work with our now-daily words.

Or, in more eloquent words from British writer Gerald Brenan: "The cliché is dead poetry. English, being the language of an imaginative race, abounds in clichés, so that English literature is always in danger of being poisoned by its own secretions."

The Grammar Damner

Here's something you will not hear at an airport departure gate: "We are now beginning preboarding for first-class passengers. All first-class passengers sit down and stay where you are."

By grammatical logic, every one of us in the gate waiting area is in first class, as we've been in a state of preboarding for that particular flight since the moment of our birth. This now-common term really means "pre-general-boarding," because once boarding begins for anyone, first class or not, you can throw the *pre-* in the trash can near the white courtesy phone. You can't take *pre-* on board. FAA rules.

Well, obviously it's my turn to be one of the persnickitors that I gripe about through this book. If I were being a proper descriptivist, the kind who defends *kudo* as a singular, I'd be sitting back in the not-so-comfy gate area and admiring delightful logic-mangling in the spirit of useful word creation. Instead, I stand up and say, "My name is Bill, and I'm a persnickitor." Sometimes, anyway. Like these times:

PLURAL'S

You do not use an apostrophe when forming plurals.

Just last evening I spotted a news story, posted on the web by a major news organization, describing a disturbance during a protest march: "Amid the cries and chaos, photographers were kicked, their camera's tossed." After seeing that sentence, my cookie's were nearly tossed.

Now, apostrophizing the word *cameras* was obviously the result of typing error and subsequent editing error (or, perhaps, of pure editorial *I-don't-give-a-damn*), and not ignorance of the language. Otherwise, both writer and editor would have standardized the sentence to refer to *cry's* (or maybe even *crie's*) and *photographer's*, and, heck, why not refer to *chao's* as a plural of a single instance of *chao*? (Also see page 148 for my discussion of *kudo* versus *kudos*, which might very well be resolved by creating the word *kudo's*.)

I suggest that lackadaisical overuse of the apostrophe is fueled by an abundance of initialisms these days, as writers try to mind their P's and Q's. (No one is quite sure why we don't watch, say, our J's and X's, but that's another story.) In the case of this hoary phrase, *minding your Ps and Qs* (or worse yet, your *ps and qs*) is potentially confusing, especially if doing so involves crossing your ts and dotting your is. Dotting I's is clearer than is dotting Is. But now everything seems to be reduced to initialisms: IMHO, TYVM, and following the pattern of crossing your P's and dotting your Q's, people regularly write of visiting MD's and listening to DJ's in the 1990's. Here, the apostrophe is by fading convention a clarifier. But *MD* and even *M.D.* is a word in and of itself, so to make it plural, add *S*. We visit MDs. Better yet, use the actual phrase. (For more on this, see my rant about *RBI* as a plural on page 39.)

The same thinking applies to dates. We increasingly refer to the 1990s and not the 1990's—and it gets especially confusing with dates when using an apostrophe to indicate contraction: We should refer to the '90s, not the 90's (and certainly not the '90's—one apostrophe to a customer, please!).

And now, returning to our cries and chaos, in case you were curious, the new's organization that reported the major breaking story of tossing cameras was . . . CB'S.

RBI

File under "Batted In, runs (*damnit*) runs!": Though the plural of *moose* is *moose,* the plural of *RBI* is not *RBI.*

Some years back, sportscasters—for reasons unclear to me—decided that a usage common in baseball needed some grandiose revisions. The plural of *RBI* (run batted in, which is of course a critical baseball stat) had been lo these many decades iterated as *RBIs*. AreBeeEye, an abbreviation, had solidified into worddom independent of its initialized components. One run batted in—one RBI. Two runs batted in. Two RBIs. (Or as one former-player-turned-announcer tiresomely and endlessly refers to them, two "ribeye steaks"—hand me the pillow so I can take a snooze.)

Oh oh!

Someone noticed that the actual word being pluralized was *run,* not *in.* *Runs* batted in. So the ruling was made, either by practice or by edict, that "Runs Batted In" should follow the lead of "Run Batted In," and also be abbreviated RBI. "Smith has 35 RBI." But doing this is almost as if the reporter is creating the initialism mid-sentence (or on the fly, as they say in both computer and baseball usages), picking three words off the shelf and without the listener or reader being aware of it, pluralizing the proper word, and *then* compacting them. (Several wags, me among them, have suggested that using this line of reasoning, the plural RsBI would be appropriate.) Instead, what the reporter should really be doing is picking the single unit—the clearly understood RBI—off the shelf and then making it plural.

Now, I see and appreciate some element of this nonconstruction. Back to baseball terminology, a batter hit by a pitched ball and awarded first base is officially a "Hit Batsman." I wonder if the "RsBI" persnickitors have questioned the possibility that this phrase might imply that the batter was using two bats, as opposed to a "Hit Batman," which describes the Tim Burton versions of the Dark Knight and not the sad Joel Schumacher "Batman Bombs" movie versions. But I digress (which you gotta be used to by now). Just today, I watched a ballgame in which more than one batter was hit by a pitch, and when commenting on that to my son, I referred to "Hits Batsman" when stumbling through my effort to form a plural. "Hit Batsmen," of course, would have been the plural (or maybe "Hit Batsmans). So I acknowledge the difficulty of speaking the clichés of a sport whose terminology is so complex that they've resorted to hand signals to communicate with each other.

Still, and back to the original subject, more than one RBI should be written as RBIs because *RBI*, despite being an initialism, is a definite verbal unit. Now—especially given the subhead of this section—you are probably wondering why I'm not applying the same logic to *moose*. More than one moose should be *mooses*. From a logical standpoint, I agree. From a standpoint of language inertia but also of language tradition, I concede that *mooses* will not be accepted.

What's more, back to the specific word unit that this essay supposedly concentrates on, the update of *RBIs* plural to *RBI* plural seems out of character—to emphasize the baseball environs, it seems to come out of left field, especially because in left field and everywhere else on the baseball diamond, the batter who has hit a pop fly leading to an out has "flied out." Few should impose real grammar on that pop-up, intoning that the batter "flew out" to left field (unless he has some pretty strong wings). And similarly, no one should be thinking that hard about the intricacies of a traditional plural in a game of tradition.

WE, MYSELF, AND I
The plural of first-person *I* is not *We.*

We shall argue about the plural nature of the word *we* from a number of standpoints. Writing these very words, we will point out to you, first, that we are employing the Technicality Defense—I (yes, I) have so far been employing "the editorial we," synonymous with *I,* so thus far the word *we* is representing the singular first person. This is also known as "the royal we," and when editors use "the editorial we," writers refer to it ultimately as "the royal-pain we."

Then, we move to the I-Defer-to-a-More-Articulate-Wag Defense, turning to Ambrose Bierce's *Devil's Dictionary*: "In grammar [I] is a pronoun of the first person and singular number. Its plural is said to be We, but how there can be more than one myself is doubtless clearer to the grammarians than it is to the author of this incomparable dictionary. Conception of two myselfs is difficult, but fine." If Bierce says such a thing about language, we are inclined to sometimes agree, but always be edified.

Then, from the technicalities to the technical. *We* is not the plural of *I,* which is the basis of Bierce's quippery. *We* is a first-person pronoun indicating that the object is plural, inclusive of the speaker and at least one other in the speaker's "group." This is a technical distinction, made even more difficult to envision because the word *I* takes singular verb forms (I think, therefore I am), while the word *we* takes the plural (We think, therefore we are).

So, technically, *we* is defined as "the pronoun of the first person plural nominative." And here we will offer something to further consider: Shouldn't *we* instead be defined as a "pronoun of the first *persons*"?

A OR AN

You are not a cockney (well, maybe you are, in which case, this book is getting wider distribution than I'd hoped).

Quick recap of the grammar involving the indefinite articles, *a* and *an:*

If the indefinite article modifies a word beginning with a vowel sound, use *an*. An apple. An herb (if you pronounce it like a bit of gastric disruption). An umpire.

If the indefinite article modifies a word beginning with a consonant, use *a*. A napple. (A napple? What's a napple? See page 122 for more information.) A herb (if you pronounce it like the first name of President Hoover, which seems to be the rage these days—herbs, not hoovers). A unicorn.

Yet, witness the title of a teleconference given through the University of Illinois, Champaign-Urbana, some time ago: "The role of grammar in communicative language teaching: An historical perspective."

That, to my eye and ear, is an hypercorrect phrasing. *Historical.* *H* is pronounced. And, again to my eye and ear, those that properly say "a historical perspective" are a honorable bunch.

CANNOT

File under "Cannot Can Not": *Cannot* is not necessarily one word; or, *cannot* isnot necessarily one word, and probably shouldnot be.

I can not deny the flow of identical consonants in the compound verb *cannot*. I also concede some fairly subtle potential differences in the elocutions: saying "You can not go" might mean, "You have the choice not to go" (though when spoken by my wife, it means I have no choice—yeah, I'm going), while "You cannot go" clearly means the only choice is staying. And then there's the matter of speaking the word(s) aloud: placing a space between the two sylla-bles introduces something of a ghost stutter when articulating the *n* twice. Yet, this joining—with no other precedent I can find (until I get that snarky letter from one of you kind folks)—is noticeably inconsistent with the other verb-nots (and you know from my comments on these pages that I am a consistency militant, though inconsistently so). As we've seen in the introduction to this section, *isnot* doesnot work (nor does *doesnot*), and *shouldnot* doesnot work, as well. Add to the list the other have-nots: *willnot, shallnot, amnot, donot, doesnot, maynot, mustnot, astronot* (just kidding).

But I amnot kidding about *couldnot.* If using *cannot* vs. *can not* is so important in distinguishing the meanings of "You are unable to go" and "You are able to opt not to go," then why don't those who insist on this distinction apply the same logic to *could not?*

"You could not go" can mean "You could choose to not go," and in fact I submit that using *could* when expressing such option is far more common than using *can.* If a teenager said, "I just scratched the car—what will I tell my dad?," his pal is more likely to reply, "Well, you could not tell him" than he would "You can not tell him." Given that greater usage, wouldn't those who insist on *cannot* even more vigorously call for bringing the nonexistent *couldnot* into the language?

Now, if it weren't for the fact that *cannot* has been in use since around the thirteenth century, I'd suggest that perhaps the conjoining of syllables is a conservationist effort, seeking to avoid expending unnecessary spaces out into, well, out into space. In this light, eschewing *can not* in favor of *cannot* could be viewed as a matter of wastenotwantnot.

The Broken Are Made to Be Rules

I admit that I need memory crutches—*mnemonics*, in the terminology—to remember spellings. Here's one I devised for the difference between *discreet* ("judicious or prudent") and *discrete* ("separated or individual"): "Lovers named E meet discreetly; but jealous T forces the E's to be discrete." Sure, it's a little silly, but with a few plot complications, I figure I can turn that into a best-selling romance novel.

Another useful mnemonic[14] that I didn't make up is "The villain lives in the villa." Good memory-nudge. Broken etymology. Villains were the farmhands that supported the villa; they probably never saw the inside of it except to wash the dishes.

So, broken can be useful as long as you don't believe every syllable. Consider the following grammar "rules" as nothing more than mnemonics, and you'll serve yourself well. They aren't rules made to be broken; they are dictates full of exceptions to the point of being broken, and unfortunately foisted upon us as rules. I.E. (that is to say) . . .

E.I.

"*I* before *E* except after *C*" is not necessarily good advice.

Oops. I fear that this entry will be mis-listed in the index. It should appear in the letter *I* section, since, as we've all been taught, ladies before gentlemen, women and children first, horse before cart, age before beauty, calm before storm, *I* before *E* except after *C*.

Except in words like *weigh* and *neighbor,* the instruction graciously allows.

---

[14] I realize as I type this that I need a mnemonic for spelling *mnemonic.*

The gracious instruction falls short.

So it's better to memorize the following bit of grammatical instruction (and there'll be a quiz when you finish the book): *I before E except after C.*

Except in words like *weigh* and *neighbor* . . . and *absenteeism* and *albeit* and *apartheid* and *atheism* and *beige* and *being* and *caffeine* and *casein* and *codeine* and *counterfeit* and *cuneiform* and *deify* and *deign* and *deity* and *dreidel* and *eider-down* and *eight* and *either* and *feign* and *feint* and *foreign* and *freight* and *geisha* and *gneiss* and *heifer* and *heigh-ho-heigh-ho-it's-off-to-work-we-go* and *height* and *heinous* and *heir* and *inveigle* and *Leicester* and *leisure* and *neigh* and *neither* and *obeisance* and *Pleistocene* and *protein* and *reign* and *rein* and *reindeer* and *reinvent* (without *reiterating* all the other potential re-suffix words) and *reveille* and *seine* and *seismic* and *seize* and *sleigh* and *sleight* and *sovereign* and *specified* and *spontaneity* and *stein* and *surveillance* and *their* and *veil* and *vein* and *weir* and *weird* and *leiyons* and *teigers* and *beirs*, oh *mei*.

So, "*I* before *E* except after *C*"? Well, sometimes. Or to follow the rule, putting the *I* before the *E* and all that, perhaps *I* should say, *somitemes.*

E.I., PART II (AND THEREFORE, I.E.)
The "*I* before *E* except after *C*" rule continues to be insufficient.

The spelling canard discussed in the entry directly above—a "*I* before *E* except after *C*"—is a niceish rule that's easy to conceive and perceive (in words like *niceish, conceive,* and *perceive*). Yet, the "except after C" part can deceive: such placement is not always *effi-cient*, in words like *ancient* and *beneficience* and *caleficient* and *calori-ficient* and *concierge* and *conscience* and *currencies* (and *frequencies* and *redundancies* and *etceteracies*) and *deficient* and *delicacies* and *fancier* and *financier* and *glacier* and *hacienda* and *omniscience* and *prescient* and *proficient* and *saucier* and *science* and *society* and *spacier* and *species* and *spicier* and *sufficient* (and *sufficiencies*, to boot!). C what *I* means?

SUBJECT-VERB AGREEMENT
Subjects and verbs, like linguists, don't necessarily have to agree.

When I note that subjects and verbs must play nice—no conflict, no disagreement, staying on the same figurative page—I'm right, aren't I?

What? I are not right?

Indeed, I are definitely not right, as evidenced that few readers took exception to the "I'm right, aren't I?" sentence above. Well, maybe *you*—you individually, the person holding this copy of this book at this moment—took exception, but did you hear anyone else speak up about it when you were reading it? I rest my case.

Now, if someone were to track me down in the hallway and insist that verbs must agree with their subjects, I would reply, "You're right," and not just because I fear that someone who would track me down to make such a point might want to elevate the argument to fisticuffs. I would then add, "Because you are right, you are wrong." The singular you "are" right? If "you are right" is right, then subjects and verbs don't necessarily have to agree, and therefore the "you" who has tracked me down in the hall is wrong (are wrong?).

Convinced? Good, because now you're wrong. "You are right" is right on historical terms, and "You is wrong" is wrong on those same terms. To learn why, thou ist invited (and y'all are invited, too) to consult the entry for "Y'all" elsewhere in this book,[15] specifically, page 165.

VOWEL RULES

File under "Two Vowels Walked into a Bar . . .": Walkin' the walk ain't necessarily talkin' the talk.

Here's a fun rule to help us with the pronunciation of double-vowel words like *roam, peak,* and *bait:* "When two vowels go walking, the first does the talking." A good rule, *albeit naive,* and sometimes a *moot* point, *said* Mr. *Caesar* the *financier.* And to borrow from another spelling rule, "except in words like *weigh* and *neighbor.*" Not to mention *mention,* or to pick out some diphthongs to make the *point.*

WHO, WHOM, WHOOMER, WHOOMEST

The "he or him" test to determine whether to use "who" or "whom" is not adequate advice.

> Knock knock.
> Whom's there?
> Meme.
> Meme whom?
> Meme, Iself and I.

---

[15] My apologies for making you jump around the text like that—*oh,* which reminds me, I shouldn't have written this footnote.

I have to admit that this is the first knock-knock joke I've ever written. I created it here not with the idea of having third-graders the world over repeat it while I bask in the influx of knock-knock-joke royalties, but to illustrate the irritating hypercorrection of the word *who*. Is the example *too* concocted? Perhaps, yet consider this fairly common real-world bastardization of *who* (which we'll call a ring-ring joke):

Ring ring.

Hello?

Is George there?

Whom shall I say is calling?

Uh . . . meme.

In the above example, *Who* would be correct, because it is the subject of the sentence, and not the object of a prepositional phrase, where *whom* would be at whome, er, home. "To whom shall I direct the call?" is correct. *Who* used as the subject of the sentence is also correct, and "Whom is at the door?" would be grammatical only if you could reconstruct it as "The door is at whom?"

And here's where we get into the myth of the "he or him" rule. This litmus test asks you to replace the *who/whom* in question with *he/him* to see what sounds right.

- George took the call from who?
- George took the call from he.

So therefore *whom* is technically correct. Note, however, that this test doesn't always work. Consider:

- Whoever took the last cookie shall die a sugary death!
- Himever took the last cookie . . . um . . .
- He-ever took the last cookie . . .

Well, looks like we have to sorta figure out for ourselves that *whoever* in the test sample is indeed correct (but I still want to find out which of my "friends" took that last cookie).

Now, if you don't want to be sexist about all this, you can instead use the "she or her" test, replacing the owlish word in question with feminine pronouns and thereby make the world a more tolerant place. Better yet, alternate equally between he/him and she/her just to make sure everyone's covered. (To show how confusing this is, I offer, without further comment, a quote attributed to a recent President: "You teach a child to read, and he or her will be able to pass a literacy test." Are you writing all this down?)

Meantime:

Ring ring.

Hello, can I put you on hold?—I think there's someone at the door.

Knock knock.

Who's there?

Whom.

Whom who?

Is that a trick question?[16]

BETWEEN

Twixt you and me . . .

"Between you, me, and the wall," he whispered, "there's a rule that *between* must be used when speaking of two, and *among* when speaking of three or more."

OK, then. Let's whisper, "Among you, me, and the wall . . ."

I rest my case.

---

[16] Please respect me for all the cheap *who/whom* jokes I resisted, like Abbott and Costello's Whom's on First baseball comedy routine, and the Internet search company Ya-whom!, and the book *Whom's Whom in America*, and the chant of my hometown Cincinnati Bengals: Whom-dey! Whom-dey! Whom-dey think gonna beat them Bengals!—well, all the cheap *who/whom* jokes that I resisted until I had to fill some space on this page with a footnote.

CONJUNCTIONS

You should not not start a sentence with *because*.

Baby Boomers will start singing along to one of the early television spelling/pun lessons when I start quoting the official song of the *Mickey Mouse Club* (the one with Annette, not Britney[17]), the one beginning, "M-I-C." And now you can hum along in your head to the rest of the song.

What a terrible lesson the Mouseketeers were giving us kiddies. K-E-Why? Because they were violating that stringent grammar rule: never start a sentence with *because*. K-E-Why? Because . . . well, I'm not sure why. I've not seen anything that offers a legitimate linguistic reason to not begin a sentence with *because* or with other conjunctions.

I picture this argument, not among us aspiring Mouseketeers on grade-school playgrounds, but among aspiring linguists supervising grade-school playgrounds:

"You should never start a sentence with *because!*"

"Why not?"

"Because."

"Because why?"

"Because you shouldn't. And never start a sentence with *and*."

"Why not?"

"Because."

"But you just started a sentence with *and*."

"Because it worked. It was an additional point, and I communicated that quickly by starting the sentence with *And*."

"Oh, so you *can* start a sentence with *and*?"

"No. You can't start a sentence with a conjunction."

---

[17] And not just because Annette was sexy, while Britney was only sexed.

"If you can't start a sentence with a conjunction, how would I
    have otherwise started *this* sentence?"
"My point exactly. And never start a sentence with *but*."
"Why not?"
"Because."

Let's consider the function of a conjunction—a nicely rhyming
phrase that sounds like it would make a good song, and indeed it
does. So let's move ahead a decade to the '70s and the venerable
Schoolhouse Rock shorts that taught us how to hum along with
curricula between Saturday morning cartoons. A song called
"Conjunction Junction" used railroad metaphors to show us how a
conjunction worked: "Hooking up two boxcars and making 'em run
right." Those boxcars, sang the singing educators, included words,
clauses, and phrases. But not sentences? Too big a boxcar?

The truth is that this is more a stylistic than a grammatical dictate.
The thinking seems to be that the conjunction must reside between
a capital letter and an ending period, isolated within a sentence, so as
to more clearly operate in connecting the sentence's components. If
a sentence is begun by a conjunction, the elements that it connects
are by definition isolated—by said princess-and-the-pea period. How
can the conjunction connect what the period separates?

This is decent logic and a strong consideration in writing
powerful prose. The more closely you can physically and mentally
draw words and thoughts together, the clearer your writing. But
nothing in grammar demands such non-separation, and in fact
separating highly connected thoughts can help writers avoid run-
ons, add muscular ripples and rhythms to the prose, and give
distinct thoughts elevated importance in distinct sentences . . . and
then driving these thusly elevated thoughts back into union with a

word that indicates relationship (*and, because*), shift (*but*), option (*or*).

However, the persnickitors would argue about . . . well, if there's anything they should argue about from their point of view, they would argue about this sentence, which begins with *however. However* being not only a synonym of the reviled sentence-starter *but,* but also a conjunction.

Simply said, a conjunction joins. Period.

Although . . .

M-I-C my point? And as not to leave you hanging . . . M-O-U-S-E!

Acronymania: Specious Histories & Ignorant Twaddle

Doesn't the acronym created by the words after the colon above say it all?[18] Most acronymic explanations of giggle-inducing words are pure (as we said on page 5) "bull"—which comes from a French word meaning nonsense with no bovine implications, until we more fully investigate our definition-establishing first entry, beginning with (don't say it aloud, keep it quiet, whisper it) shhhhhh . . .

SHIT (BLUSH BLUSH)

Our word investigator reports back that *shit* is not an acronym, to which we respond, "No shit, Sherlock."

How appropriate that the Internet neo-etymologists are spreading informational manure about the word *shit*. The supposed origin of this ancient word is "traced" (with crayons, I would suggest) to nautical transport. When hauling dried manure on board seagoing vessels (manure being the jewel of the international sea trade after all), seafarers were careful to stack said treasure atop other cargo. If the manure were to be so unfortunately placed as to soak up some water, it would release methane into the trapped space, causing a prodigious explosion should Long John Silver slip into the room for a quick surreptitious smoke, *arrh mateys!* So, anything containing potential methane-based detonators was marked S.H.I.T. to communicate the instruction, "Ship High in Transit."

First, let's tackle the logic:

---

[18] Actually, most of the stuff that the acronym spells out comes from the colon in the first place, but then again, this isn't an anatomical tract (and no pun intended on *tract,* either).

1) How often do we translate potential disaster-averting instructions to their initials, when perhaps clarity might serve us well? The signs say "Fire Exit," not "F.E." The words "This End Up," and not the initials "T.E.U.," are stamped on the sides of packing crates. "Baby on Board," and not "B.O.B." (and a good thing, too, since that sign has prevented me from intentionally ramming other vehicles numerous times—"Save the babies!"). And on and on.

2) Who's gonna stack manure on top of, oh, say, spices in the first place?

3) Wouldn't these sailors be a little more concerned about the reliability of a ship whose cargo holds might flood than the potential of said flood triggering a Rube Goldbergian series of unlikely events leading to massive detonations? You don't have to worry much about methane gas when you're 30 fathoms deep and still descending.

4) Wouldn't something more mundane and connected have a little more credibility as a source of an acronym? Like "Sit High In the Throneroom"—even that flippant concoction makes more sense than the transit nonsense.

Shit is one of a number of words assigned acronymic origins that are dubious if not ridiculous. Other such words are *posh* (see page 58), *fuck* (61), *wop* (page 67), *golf* (60), *phat* (page 67) and *tips* (65). Such acronymic concoctions are sometimes a guess at words of unknown origin. Sometimes they're tools of someone with an agenda. Sometimes they're just BS. And you can say the same about much of folk etymology.

In any case, why don't the people who make this stuff up ever select long words like *pleonasm, Machiavellian,* or *radial-keratotomy* and turn them into acronyms? Why don't they take boring common words and assign them boring origins, perhaps suggesting that *door* is an acronym of "Don't Open Our Roof" or *nose* results from "Nasal Orifice South of Eyes" or, if the source is Latin, "Noble Orifice South of Eyes"? Because such construction isn't a good line of shit. Unless the word is *shit* itself.

To help you identify such baloney-filled etymologies, consider the English Skeptic's Rules of Acronymity, otherwise known as "Specious Histories & Ignorant Twaddle":[19]

- **Rule 1 of Specious Histories & Ignorant Twaddle:** If the word is older than your great-great-grandpappy, the acronym-based etymology is false. The particular fecal word we're discussing here traces back to Old English and other Old Languages, and ultimately back to Proto-European **skei-.*[20] On the other hand, the very mechanism of creating words from the initial letters of phrases traces back to Proto-Last-Week in linguistic terms. David Wilton in his *Word Myths* writes, "There is only one known pre-twentieth-century word with an acronymic origin and it was in vogue for only a short time in 1886. The word is *colinderies* or *colinda,* an acronym for the Colonial and Indian Exposition held in London in that year." I'd like to usurp a recent word creation to define this type of word "construction." *Anacronym,* a blending of *anachronism* and *acronym,* has been defined as an acronym whose founding letters you have forgotten, like *laser,* which stands for "Light-Amplified Something or oth*ER.*" But that definition suggests the word is old, not that it's out of synch with its time—for instance, if the

---

[19] Alternate acronym sources: "Stupid Humor in Taxonomy," "Syllable Hype, Internet Trash," and "Sloppy, Hopelessly Inane Theories." By the way, I hope to spread the Internet rumor that *shit* is an acronym meaning "Shit High in Transit," and see if anyone gets the joke.

[20] Even though asterisks sometimes signal footnotes, and even though this is a footnote, the asterisk here and elsewhere identifies words that we believe existed by extrapolation rather than actual observation. Have I put you to sleep yet?

laser was mentioned in a novel set in the Renaissance. Da Vinci wasn't *that* smart. I submit that the word *anacronym* is better used to mean an acronym that, like Da Vinci's laser, couldn't possible have been part of the word's history. So, usurper that I am, let's call this one the "Rule of Anacronymy."

- **Rule 2 of Specious Histories & Ignorant Twaddle:** If the supposed source words make you blush, snicker, or belch, the acronym-based etymology is false.

- **Rule 3 of Specious Histories & Ignorant Twaddle:** If the resulting word makes you blush, snicker, or belch, the acronym-based etymology is false.

- **Rule 4 of Specious Histories & Ignorant Twaddle:** If the resulting word was spelled in different ways over time, the acronym-based etymology is false. Consider a real acronymic creation: *snafu*. People argue about the specific words that added up to *snafu*, but no one disagrees about the spelling.

- **Rule 5 of Specious Histories & Ignorant Twaddle:** If you learned about the word from the Internet, which is often no more than an electronic upgrade of mimeographs pasted on bulletin boards and scribblings on bathroom walls, the acronym-based analogy is false. Let's call this the "Rule of Bullshitternet."

- **Rule 6 of Specious Histories & Ignorant Twaddle:** If the resulting word doesn't consolidate a proper name, usually of an organization (e.g., *NATO, PETA*), it is increasingly likely that the acronym-based etymology is false.

- **Rule 7 of Specious Histories & Ignorant Twaddle:** If the resulting word is not military (such as, *AWOL, WAC, humvee, jeep,* and even, yes, *snafu*), technological (*RAM, laser*), or both (*sonar, radar*), the acronym-based etymology likely is false. I once worked for a computer consultancy, which is where I surmised that all things computer had to be boiled down to three-letter initialisms or acronyms.

> **Rule 7 of Specious Histories & Ignorant Twaddle, Corollary A:** If the origin is supposedly nautical, the acronym-based etymology likely is false. See specifically *posh* in the entry immediately following this one, but also refer again to David Wilton: "there is a tendency among some nautical enthusiasts to attribute a maritime origin to just about every word and phrase they can think of. This tendency is so common that one of the participants in the www.wordorigins.org online discussion group dubbed it CANOE, or the Conspiracy to Attribute Nautical Origins to Everything." In other words, there is S.H.I.T. in your CANOE (or perhaps more appropriately the reverse).

So, after all that, you're certainly curious about the false origin of the word *acronym*. Well, as I would note to our friends, the Internet neoetymologists, acronym is an acronym of *A Constant Repetition of Nonsense, You Moron.*

POSH

File under *"Posh!? Again!? Oh No!"*: Oh, definitely yes, once again and ad infinitum, you don't know the origin of the word *posh*.

If you've been a language-lover for any length of time, you've likely encountered suggested origins of the word *posh*. And any tome that spends any moment of time whatsoever discrediting false etymologies simply must address the subject. It's basic, it's fundamental. Kind of like lifting weights, doing stretches, and taking batting practice before the big game. *Posh* is the poster child of bad etymology. Please donate your pennies to the Campaign Against Impoverished Etymology (it's not the source of an acronym—don't try).

Better yet, please donate your half-pennies, and I'll explain why in a moment.

First, the batting practice. Toss the "Port Out Starboard Home" acronym story into the air and I'll smash it with my Louisville Slugger. Once upon a time, early in a century known as the nineteenth, rich people sailing from England bought first-class tickets that guaranteed cabins on the cooler, afternoon-shaded port side of India-bound ships, and the afternoon-shaded starboard side when England-bound. (I suspect they slept in the middle of the ship at night.) No evidence physical or reliably anecdotal confirms that such a first-class designation existed. What's more, *posh* as acronym is in almost certain violation of "Rule 1 of Specious Histories & Ignorant Twaddle," and in absolute violation of "Rule 4 of Specious Histories & Ignorant Twaddle, Corollary A" (see page 57). Hugh Rawson in *Devious Derivations* reports an alternate explanation: the "waggishly suggested Port Out Sherry Home," which even if we didn't know it as a jest, would violate "Rule 2 of Specious Histories & Ignorant Twaddle."

OK, that was easy. Any language-loving curmudgeon can get his whacks in on such an easy target. But where does the word really come from? Any ideas? I offer a penny for your thoughts. But because I'm a cheap bastard, let's make it a half-penny for your thoughts. In *A Browser's Dictionary*, John Ciardi writes that "British Gypsies commonly, if warily, worked with British rogues [who] came to know *posh* in such compounds as *posh-houri*, half pence, and *posh-kooroona*, half crown, so associating it with money." It would seem that those were obviously economically different times, when the thought of having a half penny meant you were living the good life, all posh and well-to-do. *Money? He has half-pennies to burn!* But the connection becomes clearer when considering the theory that the *påš xåra*, shortened to be pronounced "posh," took figurative meaning as money, or wealth, just as the simple word *coin* has done.

There might be another clue to *posh* in half-pennies, or as some Brits might say, "ha-pennies," swallowing a couple of letters, including *pas* of the word *pas*, or "half of the word *half*," to translate from the native Romani. Such consonant swallowing (we might say "swa'ing") perhaps led to the word *polished* being pronounced *poshed*, with the *D* being absorbed when following the word with one that begins with a consonant, a theory forwarded by J.P. Maher, Professor Emeritus of Linguistics at Northeastern Illinois University Chicago.

Any way you look at it, the origin of *posh* remains in dispute—all except for the nautical acronym fairy tale. So if someone tells you that story, reply "bosh!," a word that was not constructed from Bullshit Out, Silly History.

GOLF

Fore! heaven's sake, the word *golf* was not fore!med as an acronym.

Let's dispense with this one with as few strokes as possible: *Golf* is *not* an acronym for "Gentleman Only, Ladies Forbidden," a supposed etymology that violates just about every rule of Specious Histories & Ignorant Twaddle (see page 55). In particular, let's review "Rule 4: If the resulting word was spelled in different ways over time, the acronym-based etymology is false." The word *golf* was first recorded in the fifteenth century, with the current spelling, but the *Oxford English Dictionary* also notes that subsequent spellings included (in alphabetical and not chronological order, for purposes of reference) *goif, goiff, goff, golf* (big surprise), *golfe, golff, golph, gouff,* and *gowff.* This would suggest that the mythical anacronymizers were very busily editing their work to get the base words perfect, before deciding that their first spelling was right after all. What's more, the first of those spellings was not *golf,* but the one that might spell "Gentlemen Only, Unsuspecting Females Forbidden."

Suffice it to say that the chances of a clever or unseemly acronymic origin being correct is about as good as you shooting a hole-in-one on a Masters par 6.

FUCK (BLUSH BLUSH)

File under "Word, F-": The gutter word for sexual intercourse is not an acronym.

My second-favorite moment of television blunderdom[21] occurred during a documentary retrospective, aired on network TV during the '90s, of the Woodstock Music Festival, which was staged in the '60s. At one point, the documentary cut to Country Joe McDonald, titular head of musical group Country Joe McDonald & the Fish (he was the one who wasn't the Fish). Onstage, Country Joe shouted to the crowd: "What's that spell?!" A roaring response

---

[21] My first favorite moment? It has nothing to do with English other than the fact that English was being spoken/not spoken during the incident. But now that I've mentioned it, I can't not tell it: Andy Williams (your grandma's slick crooner and schmaltzinator of TV Christmas specials, most famous for "Moon River") was hosting an Emmy Awards program (different times, obviously). Stevie Wonder was going to sing on the program via satellite remote, but technical difficulties stepped into the live broadcast, and Stevie wasn't responding to Andy's cues. "Can you hear me?" Andy said. He tried that question a time or two by my recollection, and when he got no response, Andy asked Stevie, "If you can't hear me, can you see me?" Because this is a footnote, I leave it to you to calculate the levels of inanity in asking a blind man who can't hear you that question. (And my third-favorite TV blunderdom moment involves curmudgeonly sportscaster Howard Cosell, but I'll have to wait until I write *Everything You Know About Sign Language Is Wrong* before I can tell that story's story.

rose from the half-a-million-plus flower-powered attendees. "What's that spell?!" Another roar. "What's that spell?!" A third roar.

What the editor/director/writer/whoever of this prime-time network documentary had not included in the broadcast, either by blunderdom or by sly and deliciously demonic irreverence, was Country Joe's lead-in to the repeated spelling-bee question to the gathered listeners. "Give me an *F!*," Country Joe had first yelled at Woodstock, and the Woodstockians had shouted "*F!*" in reply. Then, "Give me a *U!*" and "Give me a *C!*" and . . . well, you can see where that was going. The documentary had picked up the legendary "Fish Cheer" when Country Joe was done requesting letters from the masses of responsive Vanna White wannabes. Therefore, right there on national broadcast TV, half a million people (minus those zoned out, looking for a bathroom or catching a nap) were yelling "*Fuck!*" And three times, no less.

Now, this is neither a spelling lesson (though it should be considering that the network, if I'm recalling correctly, was the abecedorial network ABC), nor is it a Federal Communications Commission propriety lesson. Instead, this is a lesson in concocted etymology. To explain, here are two sequences that Country Joe did not shout to the crowd:

C-Joe did not, for one, yell "Give me a 'Fornication'! Give me an 'Under'! Give me a 'Consent'! Give me an 'of the King'!"

Nor, for that matter, did C-Joe yell, "Give me a 'For'! Give me an 'Unlawful'! Give me a 'Carnal'! Give me a 'Knowledge'!" (He might have yelled that had he been backed up not by the Fish but by Van Halen, the band that released a 1991 album entitled *For Unlawful Carnal Knowledge*.)

Such cheer-leading proclamations would have dumbfounded the assembled masses almost as assuredly as the etymologies attributing the formation of the nasty-word as an acronym dumbfound word historians.

You see, the word in question can't be an acronym of such phrases as "For Unlawful Carnal Knowledge" if for no other reason than the word in question (starts with *F*, in case you've forgotten) is far older than acronymy as a neologic mechanism— the first tenet of the rules of Specious Histories & Ignorant Twaddle. Other factors explain why, in this case, folk etymology and fuck etymology are synonymous ("Folk etymology and the horse you rode in on!"): Our nasty *F*-word has been spelled in variant ways over the centuries, which would have required our industrious acronym-imaginers to be facile creative geniuses to keep concocting phrases that supported the acronym-creation theory over the years. There's *fuk* ("For Unlawful Knowledge"?— like knowing a state secret or something?), and *fucke* ("For Unlawful Carnal Knowledge Etc."?) and *fukk* ("For Unlawful Knowledge of the letter *K*"??) and my absolute favorite, *ffuck*, from a seventeenth-century manuscript: "Which made him to haue a mighty mind To clipp, kisse, & to ffuck."

What's worse than the F-word? The FF-word, of course.

GORP

File under "Trail Mixup": Don't swallow the "etymology" of *gorp* whole.

The concoction many of us know as "trail mix" indeed contains raisins and peanuts, but it's unlikely that *gorp* is, as has been suggested, an acronym of "Good Old Raisins and Peanuts."[22] More likely, the word come from a slang verb *gorp* ("to gobble or gulp"), which has been with us since around the beginning of the twentieth century (a time of more trails and fewer table manners, I suppose).

In a bizarre and specious speculation about the origin of the word in question, I ask you to keep in mind that three of the words in the supposed GORP acronym are closely related in the funny papers. Cartoonist Charles Schulz originally wanted his strip to be called "Good Old Charlie Brown," but the newspaper syndicate changed it to "*Peanuts.*" Coincidence? Eh? Ya think? Sure, that doesn't explain the *raisins,* but, hey, I have confidence that the bullshitternet etymologists out there will find a way to bring them in. Email me with the "derivation" when you get a chance.

NEWS

News does not result from a dyslexic compass.

Etymythology[23] tells us that *news* is an acronym for "North, East, West, South" (and all ships at sea!). I guess this might have worked if you were in, say, St. Louis, where you could indeed deliver news in all those directions. But what if you worked in LA? Would you be broadcasting NEKS: North, East and Kinda South?

The sources of *news* are *olds:* old usages. Fourteenth-century usages. And, yes, old and unanacronymic spellings. Like *neus* (perhaps including *up* as a direction). Or *newes,* which is perhaps

---

[22] Doesn't "Good Old Raisins and Peanuts" sound like a rousing vegetarian drinking song?
[23] A word I dearly wish *I* had made up, and whoever did, I thank you . . .

the inspiration of the directionally challenged Hitchcock movie, *North by East-West and East-South* (they shortened it before release, I suspect . . .).

TIPS

File under "Play Taps for Tips": *Tip* is not an acronym.

Supposedly, goes the canard, *tip* is an acronym of "To Insure Promptness." Not true. To tip, in thieves' slang in use by the early 1600s, was "to give or pass on" (think "tip on a horse race"). Noun use of *tip* was established by the mid-1700s. Our phrase "tip off," meaning "warn or signal," is an offshoot of this use. (As an aside, the level of irony of "tipping" coming from thieves' slang depends on just how bad the restaurant service was that day.)

William and Mary Morris once noted that "More probably *tip* is a corruption of *stipend,* 'a small payment of money,' from the Latin word *stips,* meaning 'gift.'" Intriguing speculation, though *tip* at three letters is nearly 43 percent of *stipend,* and in the world of tipping, 43 percent seems awfully generous.

The timetable of supposed creation of *tip* as an acronym places it in violation of the rules of Specious Histories & Ignorant Twaddle (see the blush-making entry on page 54). And so it is with a variant explanation, that *tips* resulted from "To Insure Prompt Service." If we are to give that word any acronymic origins, I'd prefer "To Insure Perpetuation of . . . well, of what Specious Histories & Ignorant Twaddle spells out."

SIC

File under "AA!": Another member joins Acroholics Anonymous (which can be refigured to read "Acronymics Anoholous").

Let's engage in a little word play, in the literal sense of the, um, word *play*:

POSH: You there in the back, the ancient-Latin-looking fellow. You're a new member to the group, aren't you? Welcome.

NEW MEMBER: Thank you. I am Sic.

POSH: Well, we all are sick to a certain degree, sir. That's why we're here.

NEW MEMBER: I mean, that is my name. I am a word called *Sic*.

POSH: Have we seen you before?

NEW MEMBER: Yes, but you may not have noticed me, because I'm usually cloaked in parentheses or brackets.

POSH: Ah, well—anyway, welcome, Sic. I am Posh.

TIPS: And I'm Tips.

SHIT: And I'm . . . well, just refer to my biography on page 56 of the book called *Everything You Know About English Is Wrong*.

POSH: Does our new member have anything to say tonight?

NEW MEMBER: Yes, I am Sic, and . . . *I am not an acronym!*

POSH: Bravo! Bravo!

NEW MEMBER: I'm a real word, a Latin word. Check my papers. I mean "thus" or "so." I do not mean "Spelled In Context" or "Same In Copy" or "Spelled In-Correctly" or "Said or Spelled in Context" or "Stet Its Clunkiness" or "Strudel Is Cheesy" or any of those things, just as you, my friend (pointing) are not "Port Out Starboard Home." And you (pointing) are not "To Insure Prompt Service." And you (pointing) are not "Ship High in Transit." And you (pointing) are not "WithOut Papers." And *you!* You are not "Pussy Hips Ass Twat"!

PHAT: What if I want to be?

NEW MEMBER: You're not! You're just a jocular misspelling. Me . . . me . . . I am a word! I am not an acronym, and thank you, Elephant Man! What's more, if I were an acronym, I would stand for "Stop Idiotic Coinages!"

THE CROWD: Here! Here! (Sic!) (Sic!)

Notymology, and Other Tales from the Bullshitternet

The Internet is hardly new, not in terms of providing the "histories" of words and phrases, nor in the context of "fascinating facts," "Did You Know!!!!?s" and other "just-how-gullible-areyou?s." Sure, the computer-to-computer linkages are latetwentieth-century, but the dissemination of specious *gosh-wows!* has a long history involving bulletin boards (pay close attention to the first syllable of that phrase), mimeograph machines, games of "telephone," and campfire tales—and probably cave drawings, as well (*Is that a picture of an alligator in a prehistoric sewer?*). The Internet is simply a far more efficient etymythology tool than its predecessors. (On the other hand, a caution regarding the modern incarnation of the bullshitternet: If it comes to you in email, distrust it. Even if you really need that hair-growth formula. It doesn't work. Trust me.)

So the specific communications process is moot—electrons or not, it's all bullshitternet, and here we'll discuss some of the claims that this ancient net has delivered to us. First, a roundup of inter-not-ymologies—claims and explanations and *wide-eyed!* "truths"—recently circulated on the Internet, in no particular order, and then we'll dive into a few specifics about specious word histories.

BULLSHITTERNETISMS
"Online" often means "off-base."

If any of the following claims pop up on your screen while you're online, disregard them, or—if you believe them—forward me your social security number and all your passwords:

- **315 entries in Webster's 1996 Dictionary were misspelled.** Cool. Which Webster's? The Webster's name is in the public domain, meaning I could have called this book *Webster's Bitching About English—could* have, but my editor rejected it for some reason. And as the name is in the public domain, there were probably at least 315 different Webster's dictionaries published in 1996. Could have been the same word misspelled in each.

- **Dreamt is the only English word that ends in the letters "mt."** Wow. Almost true. The *Oxford English Dictionary* also includes *crommt*, meaning "crooked." I use *crommt* daily, anyway. Or at least I dreamt I did.

- **Early politicians told assistants to "go sip some ale" and listen to people's conversations and political concerns to gauge the mood of the electorate. The two words "go sip" were eventually combined when referring to the local opinion, and thus we have the term "gossip."** Yeah yeah yeah. The word *gossip* has been around since the eleventh century, a time when the political machine (1) was not as sophisticated as what's described here and (2) did not exist. Not many elections in eleventh-century England. For those who believe the "go sip some ale" explanation, I say, Go sip yourself.

- **Ernest Vincent Wright's 1939 novel GADSBY has 50,110 words, none of which contains the letter "e."** True enough, but I suspect that this feat didn't occur by accident. "Say, Ernie," writes his editor, "did you realize that there aren't any *E*'s in your book? Thanks! We sold all the *E*'s you didn't use on eBay." *Gadsby* was a stunt—an exercise in wordplay known as a *lipogram*—a piece of writing intentionally avoiding a specific letter. We can't be amazed by feats achieved with such specific purpose as to warrant a name. Wright's *E*-less lipogram isn't th only novl-lngth work avoiding that partic- ular vowel; in fact, *La Disparition*, a Frnch novl not using th fifth lttr of th alphabt, was translatd into Nglish as *A Void* (and th translation also A Void'd th fifth ltter). And, sorry to say, poor Mr. Wright's verbal stunt was sabotaged by his own byline, which contains three instances of the letter *E*.

- **The expression "three dog night" originated with the Eskimos and means a very cold night—so cold that you have to bed down with three dogs to keep warm.** To that, I sing, "Liar!" Well, that's the name of one of my favorite songs from the very successful band Three Dog Night, which took its name from the *Australian Aboriginal* custom. No Eskimos. So the etymology is close, if you consider "the other side of the Pacific Ocean" as being close.

- **The first English dictionary was written by Samuel Johnson in 1755.** Well, Johnson's dictionary was *published* in 1755, meaning that Johnson would have to have been a very quick writer to have also written it in that year. Actually, Johnson's *A Dictionary of the English Language* took nine years to write. Johnson's work very well could have been the first English dictionary published in calendar year 1755, but it was hardly the first overall. The first English-only dictionary appeared 151 years earlier: Robert Cawdrey's *A Table Alphabeticall*. Sixty-six years earlier than Cawdrey, Sir Thomas Elyot's Latin-English word compendium was published. Johnson wrote the first *comprehensive and truly influential* dictionary, perhaps, but the first? No. (And the word *dictionary* itself? First recorded use was in 1526.)

- **In England, in the 1880's, "pants" was considered a dirty word!** Oh! An exclamation point! Any potential Victorian consternation about the word *pants* isn't particularly surprising, considering that unlike in the States where pants are trousers, in England pants are panties. If the English were indeed upset by the word at that time, they were hardly reacting to trousers. I mean, They were hardly reacting to trousers!

- **The computer term "byte" is a contraction of "by eight."** Hmm. There's considerable speculation on this one. Perhaps *byte* is simply a modification of a previous computer term, *bit*. One suggestion is that eight bits of information comprise the smallest unit a computer can *bite*, with a computer-geeky spelling change to make it official (just short of g33ky 133t-speak). *The Barnhart Concise Dictionary of Etymology* allows the possibility of an acronym: *b(inar)y (digi)t e(ight)*, though that seems a bit clumsy. The coinage is attributed to IBM employee Dr. Werner Buchholz in 1956, and I've seen a claim that IBM employees described a *bit* as a *bi(inary digi)t* and a *byte* as a *b(inar)y t(upl)e*. So the acronym explanation may simply be a post-creation way of keeping bits and bytes separate in people's minds, a mnemonic rather than an etymology.

- **Only four words in English end in "dous": tremendous, horrendous, stupendous, and hazardous.** Well, those four and more than 150 other words, most of them technical terms. This bull-shitternetism results from a corruption of an Isaac Asimov word puzzle in which he presented three *common* words ending in *-dous*—the positive *tremendous* and *stupendous*, and the negative *horrendous*—and then asked for a fourth, another negative. Answer: *hazardous*, although other writers have also suggested that *jeopardous* might be common enough to supply a fifth. And myself, I like *blizzardous*.

- **The original name for butterfly was flutterby.** Cute, but stupid.

- **No word rhymes with month.** Wrong! *Orange* rhymes with *month*.

- **No word rhymes with orange.** Wrong! See above.[24]

---

[24] See also *silver* and *purple*. Those two and *orange* and *month* all rhyme. Honest! I read it on the Internet!

- **The phrase "rule of thumb" is derived from an old English law which stated that you couldn't beat your wife with anything wider than your thumb.** Oh, please. This one is another quintessential bit of disinformation, misinformation, or pure mischief, depending on the reteller's motive. The phrase reflects the natural tendency to measure things according to the most readily available measuring sticks— human body parts. Thus *foot* and *cubit* (the length of your arm from the elbow down, and what Noah used to measure the Ark—and eventually build it, even though a cubit is [rim shot, please] "all thumbs"), and in greater poetic contexts, losing by a nose or a hair. If the "English law" would allow us to beat the people who propagate such nonsense with things wider than our thumb, I'd be quite happy.
- **It is believed that Shakespeare was 46 around the time that the King James Version of the Bible was written. In Psalms 46, the 46th word from the first word is shake and the 46th word from the last word is spear.** Once again, who thinks this stuff up? And what does it mean? That if we look for the forty-fifth word from the front and the forty-fifth from the back that we'll find the last name of another great writer who was forty-five at the time the King James Version was "written" (it was published in 1611, after seven years of translation)? God moves in mysterious ways, but I suspect He has better things to do. (This relates to speculation that Shakespeare, who had connections with KJ of KJV fame, might have been an unnamed contributor to the monumental translation.)
- **"Quisling" is the only word in the English language to start with "quis."** Well, there's the word *quis,* for one, though that's slang. Better yet is *quisquilian,* from a Latin root meaning "rubbish."

- **There are six five words in the English language with the letter combination "uu."** **Muumuu, vacuum, continuum, duumvirate and duumvir, residuum.** "Six five"? Let's be precise, now. Besides, the claim is a bit thorny, like the carduus thistle. And we could also add *individuum*, and other words in perpetuum.
- **The plastic things on the end of shoelaces are called aglets.** OK, sometimes the "Did You Know!!!!?" crap gets it right. Yes. Aglets.
- **Alma mater means bountiful mother.** Wow! Two for two!
- **In Scotland, a new game was invented. It was entitled Gentlemen Only Ladies Forbidden. . . . and thus the word GOLF entered into the English language.** OK, I cover this on page 60, but I wanted to take the opportunity to snark at "a new game was invented." So much easier to invent old games. And "entering into" is far more efficient than "entering out of."
- **Sheriff came from Shire Reeve. During early years of feudal rule in England, each shire had a reeve who was the law for that shire. When the term was brought to the United States it was shortned to Sheriff.** I appreciate the matching of form and content with "shortned" (it's halfway to being *Gadsby*-esque). And the *shire reeve* part is right, tracing back to Old English. But *sheriff* is but one of many spellings used for the word, including *sheref* around 1400, a year or two before there was a United States, and even before English speakers stood on future U.S. shores.
- **The sentence "The quick brown fox jumps over the lazy dog" uses every letter of the alphabet.** Considering that this classic keyboarding exercise was created specifically to include every letter of the alphabet, why does this come as a surprise to anyone? And *"Did you know that the number 1,234,567,890 contains every single-character numeral!?!?"* [25]

---

[25] Good thing nobody in *Gadsby* had to take a typing test using that sentence.

- **The oldest word in the English language is "town."** An old word indeed, but do you have a confirming birth certificate so we can send a card?
- **The language Malayalam, spoken in parts of India, is the only language whose name is a palindrome.** Well, it's not English, but what the hell. And it may be right. But who cares? Unless every word in the language is also a palindrome. Now that would be kind of cool.
- **There are two words in the English language that have all five vowels in order: "AbstEmIOUs" and "fAcEtIOUs."** There they are: *A, E, I, O, U* . . ."But what about the sometimes *Y*?," Tom Swift said facetiously. Actually, this Internet factoid is not wrong, in that it doesn't claim that there are *only* two words, and indeed there are many others: *absentious; anemious; anelidous; arsenious; arterious; assention-court*; and the group of *appendicious, appetitious, arenicolous, arreptitious,* and *atramentitious* (if you allow duplicated vowels, yet still in proper order). And that's just the *A*'s. This is like saying that there are two sentences in the history of literature beginning with the word *the*.[26]
- **The word "biology" was coined in 1805 by Jean-Baptiste Lamarck.** Bullshitternetisms aren't always ridiculous; this one may be simply out of date. *Biology* was coined in 1802 by a German, Gottfried Reinhold. Lamarck, a Frenchman, used the word in *Hydrologie*, published three years later. The word was first used in English in its present sense in 1819 (and in 1813 in the sense of studying the lives and character of humans).
- **There is a word in the English language with only one vowel, which occurs six times: Indivisibility.** Well, if we're going to play that game, how about *disindivisibility*? And, by the way, what's the *Y* in both words if not a vowel?

---

[26] And, by the way, *duoliteral* has all the vowels in reverse alphabetical order. Post *that* on the Internet!

- **The word millionaire was first used by Benjamin Disraeli in his 1826 novel *VIVIAN GREY*.** Lord Byron mentioned the term in an 1816 letter from France, and at that time the French word *millionaire* had been in use for about a century.
- **Underground is the only word in the English language that begins and ends with the letters "und."** Well, that's wrong, too, but then again, who gives a damn?
- **The book *Everything You Know About English Is Wrong* contains no references to the platypus.** Damn! I just blew that one.

JIFFY

A *jiffy* is not a small *jiff*.

I find it ironic that the first recorded use of the word *jiffy* (and in plural, no less), is in *Baron Munchhausen's Narrative of His Marvellous Travels and Campaigns in Russia (Humbly Dedicated and Recommended to Country Gentlemen)*, by Rudolf Erich Raspe. The book collects the tall tales of Hieronymous Karl Friedrich von Munchhausen, gentleman, soldier, and yarn-spinner. Among the marvellous travels are a trip to the moon on a beanstalk, and a really quick chariot ride from "just between the Isle of Wight and the main land of England" to the Rock of Gibraltar. How quick? According to a frequently repeated Internet "Did You Know!!!!?" trivial edification, precisely .06 seconds. "In short, having given a general discharge of their artillery, and three cheers, I cracked my whip, away we went, helter skelter, and in six jiffies I found myself and all my retinue safe and in good spirits just at the rock of Gibraltar."

The irony I bask in, of course, is that many Internet "Did You Know!!!!?" trivia edifications are about as plausible as the good

Baron out-beanstalking Jack all the way to the moon. And the particular edification I'm referring to has tall tale written all over it, though employing some deceptive truth:

A "jiffy" is an actual unit of time for one one-hundredth of a second!

Yes, the word *jiffy* has been used to designate a unit of time, though the specific unit varies by usage and even by scientific discipline. It's generally used to denote a hundredth of a second, as the Internet post indicates. It's also apparently been used to mean a fiftieth of a second, a sixtieth of a second, a millisecond, a nanosecond, and 33.3564 picoseconds (or a "light centimeter"—the time it takes light to travel a centimeter, by analogy of light year). However, the exclamated Internet post is lying by implication: it's set up to have the reader assume that the scientific word was used figuratively to create a vague and hyperbolic *jiffy*, as in "I'll be there in a jiffy," when the opposite is true. Most of the measurements I list above are related to computer cycles or functions. The six jiffies that expire during marvellous travel from point of origin to the Rock of Gibraltar by the good Baron were referenced in a book published in 1785, a time when—I believe it's safe to say—computer use equaled its lowest point.

So, "*A 'jiffy' is an actual unit of time for one one-hundredth of a second!*" is one of those eye-rollingly unamazing amazing facts, somewhat on the order of "A 'mouse' is an actual computer device!"

Now, for those who would have you believe that the original *jiffy* was a scientific measurement, let me say that we actually don't know where the word came from (slang to describe lightning has been suggested, and I like the poetry that that suggests), but we do know that the word *jiffy* has been in use for upwards of 7.305099E+11 jiffies (at this writing). I believe that his quite fabulous figure would make the good Baron proud.

PUMPERNICKEL
We suspect Napoleon had other things to worry about.

Here's a retort I'd like to use for some spreaders of false etymology: some people claim that the word *pumpernickel* came about when Napoleon scowled at the bread he'd been served and said "C'est pain pour Nicole," his unfortunate horse, who likely preferred its wheat and oats in less processed form. My retort: "You say it's 'pain pour Nicole'? Blow it out your ass!" Which is what you do with pumpernickel. Sort of. The origins of *pumpernickel* trace back to a German verb *pumper,* meaning "to pass gas." Something we wouldn't want poor Nicole to do.

SOS
SOS does not stand for "Save Our Ship."

It stands for "Squirrels on Sale." Well, that would make almost as much sense.

SOS stands for 911.

911 stands for *SOS.*

Both mean "Help!"

SOS was an international call for help adopted in 1908, in a time when radio messages were delivered voicelessly via Morse Code, a series of long and short clicks known as dashes and dots.

The previous distress signal was *CQD,* which posed some inherent problems because folk etymologists at the time couldn't come up with a snarky phrase to claim it was based on. Or maybe there were some real reasons that the International Radio

Telegraph Convention wanted to change the signal. Any way you look at it, it's not like the members of that Convention were sitting around trying to come up with catchy phrases in Morse Code to entertain each other. Can you imagine: "How about 'La Bamba'? When you tap the name out in Morse Code, it's got a good beat and you can dance to it."

"Wait! No! I got it. SOS. It could stand for 'Save Our Ship' or 'Save Our Souls' or 'Scrub Our Sink' when we sell the name to the scouring pad manufacturer or 'Stop Other Signals' or . . ."

"Or 'Port Out, Starboard Home'!"

No. The sequence was used because it was simple to remember, simple to tap out in urgent situations, simple to understand on the receiving end: three dots, three dashes, then three more dots. In Morse Code, that sequence coincidentally spells out SOS. Just like the numbers 911, they are symbolic of nothing, duplicative of nothing, but meaning *everything* to the people using it. Meaning everything, *except,* of course, "Squirrels on Sale."

SNOB
Snobs are not "without nobility."

The moderately common etymology seems to make sense: The Latin phrase *sine nobilitate* means "without nobility." Contract it— s(ine)nob(ilitate)—and you get our wonderful word for a pretentious pretender or a just-plain-old snooty person. And, heck, the word rhymes with *mob*, which does indeed come from a Latin phrase: *mobile vulgus*, meaning "moveable, mobile or changeable masses." The rabble.

But *snob* is first recorded in the late 1700s as a slang word of unknown origin, meaning "cobbler," not the dessert but the shoemaker. It was later used pejoratively, as are a number of words that result from "low" professions (now, I respect the folks who make shoes, as I use said devices almost daily, but on the other hand, I do have to admit that those shoemaker folk do work pretty "low"—generally at toe level).

Ironically, *snob* is a word of the mobile vulgus, and *mob* is a word of the snobs.

So, anyone who suggests to you that the word *snob* has Latin origins is himself a modern-day snob, and deserves a boot in the seat of the pants with your snob-craft.

SCAERMLBD WORDS

"I awlyas tghuhot slpeling was ipmorantt!" is not particularly insightful.

Can you read these words?:

• *ervey*
• *raed*
• *pclae*

Old English? Nope. Old Bullshitternet, tracing to 2003, which in the Internet world is the equivalent of Old English. Here's the post that these words are drawn from:

> Can you read this? Olny srmat poelpe can. I cdnuolt blveiee taht I cluod aulaclty uesdnatnrd waht I was rdanieg. The phaonmneal pweor of the hmuan mnid, aoccdrnig to a rscheearch at Cmabrigde Uinervtisy, it deosn't mttaer in waht oredr the ltteers in a wrod are, the olny iprmoatnt tihng is taht the frist and lsat ltteer

be in the rghit pclae. The rset can be a taotl mses and you can sitll raed it wouthit a porbelm. Tihs is bcuseae the huamn mnid deos not raed ervey lteter by istlef, but the wrod as a wlohe. Amzanig huh? yaeh and I awlyas tghuhot slpeling was ipmorantt!

This post is cheating you. Yes, it's remarkably understandable, if not precisely "readable." But far more factors than simply the first and the last letter in their proper positions contribute to your understanding.

First, consider the hidden familiarity of some of these wrods. Who hasn't transposed the *o* and the *r* in *word* while typing at least once? (I literally did so once while composing this entry.) Who hasn't typed *taht* instead of that? These are mistakes, but mistakes that we know and recognize. (And perhaps even accept—note the rise of the "word" *teh* as an informal and often intentional alternate of *the* on the Internet—and see page 215 to be frightened by that.) There are many simple transpositions in this post, transpositions that are easily reswapped mentally.

Next, consider the absolute familiarity of surrounding words. *Can* in the first scrambled sentence, and *I* and *was* in the second, for example. Our most common, most functional, and most powerful words are short, and difficult to disguise using the rules of this game.

Further consider that the post is rife with clues to meaning. The paragraph is punctuated as a normal English sentence, from sentence-beginning signal Capital Letters to sentence-ending punctuation signals.?! Throw in the occasional logical comma (though a semicolon in one place would lend some grammar to the nonsense), and an actual paragraph begins to take shape. Even the lone apostrophe is planted in a logical place—*deosn't* is hardly the alien counterpart of *doesn't*.

Other clues: capitalizing the improperly jumbled proper nouns: Cmabrigde Uinervtisy. Sentence construction and flow. Blatantly correct functional words (articles, conjunctions, pronouns, and so on, again, always short and unscramble-able in the rules of this game). Not many truly long words.

In regard to the latter point, how about if we were to jumble a common word to create the scrambled word *slaybells?* "Slaybells ring, are you list'nin'?" Just as the word *list'nin'* in the above lyric from "Winter Wonderland" disguises the number of syllables in the original word, *slaybells* fools us into perceiving only two syllables when the source word had three. And the source word, of course, is *syllables*. The bullshitternet post plays no such tricks.

And an additional factor is not a clue, but a motivator. "Can you read this? Olny srmat poelpe can." That's a challenge. You'll make this passage understandable if it takes you all week to translate it, even if it's as opaque as a soduku with one number in it.

But perhaps most important to this post's understandability: Context. Context. Context. Let's return to the words that began this entry: *ervey, raed,* and *pclae.* You likely stumbled over them in their isolated list, and then breezed over them when they appeared in the post istlef (sic).

Context context context. The surrounding words, the surrounding discussion, even the shape of language itself. I once ticked off a friend as we watched *Wheel of Fortune* together. The puzzle displayed a long phrase in blank letters and spaces. The purpose of the game is to guess, one at a time, what letters might fit the puzzle until you can guess the phrase. I didn't guess this particular long phrase. I knew it. And announced it before a single letter was revealed. "This must be a rerun!" she fumed. I shrugged, and said, "Language has shape," and that long phrase revealing no clues except how many letters were in each of its components had displayed its shape to me. But even during this *Wheel of Fortune* game, context ruled. I knew the general subject area because they announced the category/theme when the empty board was revealed. And I knew the phrase had to be idiomatic. Such context and shape allowed me to "read" absolutely blank letters.

And now that I have perhaps convinced you that this post is pure bullshitternet, I will, in the spirit that everything you and I know about English is wrong, point out that it's right.

Our minds do indeed regard words as units, and not as character trains, the way we regard the Taj Mahal as a magnificent building and not as a series of individual doorways, domes, and spires. In fact, a problem I see in politically correct re-speechification is that "agenda-enhanced" persnickitors view some words as a stack of individual domes instead of a separately perceived structure (see my discussion of Fishkill, New York, on page 93, as an example). It's just that the Internet post plays with you by suggesting that you could upend the domes and spin them about, lay spires on their sides and hide them under the couch cushions, and align all the doorways in a row until they form a grandiose hallway, and still call the jumble the Taj Mahal.

So, the post is right, and it's wrong and (*oh, stop it, Bill* . . .) it's wrong again. Sort of.

As with most Internet posts, the source is specious: there is no Cambridge University study or sutdy or sdtuy. It seems that the ultimate source was a PhD thesis from a Nottingham University student, by name of Graham Rawlinson, who in 1999 wrote a letter to *New Scientist* magazine about said thesis. Rawlinson concluded the letter:

> The resaon for this is suerly that idnetiyfing coentnt by paarllel prseocsing speeds up regnicoiton. We only need the first and last two letetrs to spot chganes in meniang.

> This was not easy to type![27]

EPONYMS
There's but nominal truth in eponymy.

With the intent of making a point about word histories (with an outside shot of one of the major media companies seeing this as a charming conglomeration of historical characters providing the stuff of an animated movie or at the very least a graphic novel), let me gather a cast of characters into a joke:

> *An inventor, a Philadelphia entrepreneur, a doctor, and a Civil War general walk into a bar.*

> The barkeep says, "What can I get you gentlemen?"

> "I'd like some of me," says the Philadelphia entrepreneur.

> The general nods. "One of me, as well. Two if you know where I might find me."

> "Good idea," agrees the doctor. "And since I'll be accompanying the good general, I'd like to purchase a couple of me, as well."

> The bartender says, "What the hell are you guys talking about?"

---

[27] Tell that to *my* typesetters, Mr. Rawlinson!

"Oh, never mind," huffs the entrepreneur. "Just give me some rotgut whiskey."

The general says, "Know where I can find a prostitute?"

"And do you sell prophylactics here?" says the doctor.

The bartender is appalled. "We don't have any of those things here, gentlemen!"

"None at all?" the inventor says finally. He angrily spits out, "Me!"

The bartender is agitated by now. "Just who do you guys think you are, anyway?"

Says the entrepreneur: "I'm Philadelphia distiller E.C. Booz."

The military man stiffly says, "I am Union General Joseph Hooker."

Says the doctor, "Dr. Condom here."

When the bartender insists that no *me*'s are available at his establishment, the inventor snaps again, "Oh me!"

The bartender looks at the inventor. "'Me!'? Don't tell me . . . you're the inventor of the Valveless Water Waste Preventer."

"Thomas Crapper at your service!"

That little tale is as fictional as the etymologies involving the characters' names. Supposedly, these mostly real persons lent their names to the items they were seeking in the bar. However, we knew of *booze* long before the coincidentally (and perhaps fortuitously intentionally) named whiskey distiller E.C. Booz sold hooch in the cabin-shaped bottles of the early and mid 1800s. There's no evidence of a Dr. Condom, though the device is often said to be named after said seventeenth- or eighteenth-century physician. Prostitutes were called *hookers* before the army of loose-moraled General Hooker was accompanied by concubine camp followers,[28] and the word *crap* was in use before Mr. Crapper developed a patent for a toilet flushing device in 1882.

Now, my first draft of this story was quite a bit bawdier, but I bowdlerized it to make it more suitable for a family audience, employing the process that was indeed named after a real person, Thomas Bowdler, famous for his editing Shakespeare into G-rated productions in *The Family Shakespeare* in 1818 ("To G or to PG—*that* is the question"). Yes, a number of words result from surnames of persons both real and otherwise.

This is similar to the law of Specious Histories & Ignorant Twaddle (see page 56). If the person's name makes you snicker, it's unlikely that the name was the source of our present word. If the supposed source person's name is boring, the etymology is more likely to be correct: Mr. Bowdler (*bowdlerize*); the Speverend Rooner—er, the Reverend William Spooner (*spoonerism*, from around the turn of the twentieth century); the fictional Mrs. Malaprop (*malapropism* from an 1830 play); Union General Ambrose Everett Burnside (*burnsides*, and later *sideburns*, from the 1800s); Nicolas Chauvin (*chauvinism*, from the mid 1800s); Thomas Derrick (*derrick*, because his name became associated with his tool, the gallows); Capt. Charles Cunningham Boycott (self-explanatory, from around 1880); Capt. Charles Lynch (self-explanatory, from the early 1800s);[29] Louis Pasteur (*pasteurize*, late 1800s); Massachusetts governor Elbridge Gerry (*gerrymander*, early

---

[28] This military man also did not create the phrase, "Make love, not whore."

[29] Seems like the best way to put your last name into common usage is to change your first name to "Captain Charles."

1800s); James Thomas Brudenell (the Earl of Cardigan, who likely was not wearing a sweater while he led the legendary Charge of the Light Brigade, but still got one named after his stomping grounds).

Two challenges to the "boring" rule, however, are the shepherd hero of a sixteenth-century poem who gave us the name of something the Civil War general sought to prevent with the device of the good doctor (the poem being "Syphilis, sive morbus Gallicus"), and the real-life Mrs. Amelia Bloomer, who advocated use of one of the garments the Civil War general would seek to invade—the bloomer dress, or *bloomers*.[30]

BUG, COMPUTER
Etymology is not the study of insects . . . oh, wait, yes it is.

On the Regis Philbin rendition of the game show *Who Wants to Be a Millionaire?*, a contestant won his million by identifying the physical bug that *supposedly* (a word the program did not use but should have) created the name for a computer glitch or malfunction: a moth. The contestant got his million, even though the question itself had more than one a bug in it: moths and the bugs within computers are only tenuously connected.

A false tale claims that the word's origin results from an electro-mechanical computer malfunction back in 1947 caused by a two-inch moth fouling a relay. Indeed, said moth fouled said relay and caused said malfunction. The technicians who discovered the dead moth playfully taped it into a logbook, and labeled it "First actual case of bug being found." It was a joke. And a good one, I might add.

The technicians were obviously well aware of the meaning of *bug*, slang that had been well established before the discovery of the

---

[30] Technically, we should call this garment *millers*, because Amelia Bloomer was not the inventor, but simply the advocate of a garment created by Mrs. Elizabeth Miller.

"actual" bug. In a letter written a few years before the moth incident, a scientist describing the process of product development
wrote: "this thing [the invention] gives out and [it is] then that
'Bugs'—as such little faults and difficulties are called—show themselves and months of intense watching, study and labor are requi-
site before commercial success or failure is certainly reached."
Actually, that was written not just a few years but a few decades
before the computer mishap: in late 1878.

We still aren't sure how this engineering slang originated. One
suggestion has been that it did indeed relate to the idea of an
insect sneaking into the machinery and gumming things up. And
Michael Quinion in *Ballyhoo, Buckaroo and Spuds* reports: "An
electrical handbook from 1896 suggests it was first used in
telegraphs as a joke that suggested noisy lines were caused by
bugs getting into the cables." Other, more reasonable, suggestions are that the term came from or was influenced by
nineteenth-century slang use of *bug* to describe someone
obsessed (and, by extension, *buggy,* "crazy"), or that it came from
or was influenced by a *bug* word that goes all the way back to Old
English: *bwg,* now spelled *bug,* meaning "hobgoblin."

And what's the other thin connection between the moth and an
engineering "bug"? The scientist whose 1878 letter was quoted
above was a gentleman who gave us infinite power to attract moths:
Thomas Edison, inventor of the moth-seducing light bulb.

BARBECUE
File under "Q, Barba" (or better yet, "Q, Bubba"): The word
barbecue is not from France, Texas, or the local pool hall (or, for
that matter, from a pool hall in Paris, Texas).

One of my passions is barbecue, and the very word stirs loudly voiced claims about what is true barbecue. *Barbecue is burgers on the grill! Barbecue is hours of smoking with indirect heat! Barbecue is a sloppy-joe hamburger mess on a bun! It ain't barbecue if it ain't pork!* (for you in the east), or *brisket!* (for you westward), or . . .

Etymologists with a taste for 'que make similar varying yet "definitive" claims about the true origin of the word *barbecue,* even though that origin is pretty clearly established. First, let's smoke out the purely fanciful definitives:

One claim is that grilled or smoked meat was served in drinking establishments, particularly those with such entertainments as pool tables. The place, the drink, the fun was enhanced by the food, which became known as *bar-beer-cue.* Nonsense, of course. Name me one other food (or any other thing) that has been constructed by such compounding. That's like saying "peanuts and Crackerjack" (I don't care if I never get back) could likely have been named "ballpark-beerbat." (Or, if you live in Cincinnati with its Germanic origins, the word *bratwurst* might have resulted from a typical baseball season: "bad-to-worse-with-beer-in-between"). Granted, there's a splash of alcohol in the origin of the word *barbecue,* as we'll see in a moment, but it seems that this "etymology" was concocted by someone who spent too much time with the first two syllables of *barbeercue.*

And then there's the tale that a Texan was so proud of his "Q" that he named his ranch the Bar B Q. Ignore the cuteness of the story for the moment and concentrate on the Catch-22 here. How could this clever Texan name his ranch after a style of food that was at the time unnamed because he had not yet named his ranch? And back to the cuteness, we might as well claim that the word came about because Ken first met Barbie at an outdoor cookout, grilling pork steaks, and Ken said, "Hey, Barbie's cute!"

More common than these "theories" is the contention that *barbecue* comes from the French. *Barbe* means "beard," and *queue* means "tail." When one cooks a hog whole on a spit, you cook it from "beard to tail," from barbe a queue. *Barbequeue*. Granted, there are dishes that are named according to how they're prepared, such as pot roast, though to follow the pattern of *barbe a queue,* we'd have to call it something like *compléterpourbaserdansunvraifourchaud* (my likely bad translation to French from "top to bottom in a real hot oven"). But even if we would give such a word creation mechanism any credence, consider two things: (1) Wouldn't *mouseau-a-queue* ("snout to tail") have been a more logical way of expressing the cooking method? (2) Have you ever seen a pig with a beard? Even a French pig? Little goatee, curling handlebar mustache? *Soo-oui-oui!?*

The real story, and a well-documented one at that,[31] is that Spanish explorers coming to the Americas encountered Haitian and Guyanese natives drying meats on raised platforms the Haitians called "barbacoa" (from a word in the Arawak tongue Taino) and the Guyanese called "babricots." The Spanish adopted the Haitian word, which eventually was picked up with different spelling in English. There's some contention that the word more precisely comes from *barabicu,* a Taino word meaning "sacred fire pit," but either way, we're still grillin' in the Caribbean. A backyard grill is to this day known as a barbacoa in Spanish.

And the splash of alcohol? The Haitians also roasted meat over the barbacoa frameworks, basting it in wine. So, next time you have a backyard picnic, replace the cold ones with some whites and reds

---

[31] Documentation includes discussion in a book called *The Grill of Victory,* by . . . hey! I wrote it!

and rosés, throw a table and some cues in the pool, and call the
event a *bar-vino-cue.*

KILL
Fishkill, New York, is not a piscine slaughterhouse.

In 1996 the village of Fishkill, New York, received a formal request
from the People for the Ethical Treatment of Animals (PETA) to
change the village's name to something less violent. "Fishsave" was
the specific suggestion.[32] PETA had assumed (or had pretended to
assume) that *kill* was the time-worn English word for "to murder"
(from the 1300s), when in fact it is the not-so-time-worn Dutch
word for "river, streambed, creek," brought into English in the
1600s, in particular related to the European exploration of the
Americas.

By the way, Fishkill is near other locations sporting the stream-
related syllable, including Catskill (as in Mountains), Beaverkill,
and Casperkill. As for the latter, are there any organizations worried
about the suggestion of cruelty to friendly ghosts? Or to the fact that
it's difficult to kill a ghost?

TESTIFY
File under "Witness, Bearing False": *Testify* does not mean . . .
well, you'll see.

I swear that the "attested" etymology of the word *testify* concerning
a certain placements of the hands to signal veracity is wrong, and I

---

[32] I like "Fishcoddle" better—might even sound kinda sorta like *Fishkill* in the spirit of the
nonsense of the name change. Rhymes with "Fishtwaddle," too, for whatever that's worth.

do so without covering my groin with my hands. My pants do the job nicely, thank you.

So, what's all that about? Placement of the hands? Groin? We're obviously not talking about putting your left hand on the Bible while raising the right to swear to tell the truth, the whole truth, and nothing but the truth. We're talking about the etymology that has no truth, no whole truth, and nothing to do with the truth: the claim that *testify* results from an ancient Roman practice of averring truth when under oath by covering one's genitals (if you're a guy, anyway—as *testify* is obviously related to *testes* or *testicles*).

In fact, there is a connection between *testes* and *testify*, though sorting through the theories of exactly what that connection is has all the excitement of a courtroom transcription. Let's jump to the closing arguments and simply point out that the Latin word *testis*, "witness," which led directly to the word *testify*, came before any application of the word to things now testicular. One theory, in fact, is that *testis* may have been borrowed to describe gonads as figurative witnesses to virility.

The fascinating sidelight to all this is that the word *testis* ultimately derives from two Indo-European roots, *tre-* and *sta-*, meaning "three" and "stand" respectively. The idea is that someone who testifies is a third party who can provide a disinterested point of view. The thought that *testicles* ultimately derives from a root meaning "three" presents an odd bit of biological irony.[33]

HONEYMOON
Someone was not sober when they made up this etymology.

---

[33] Nowadays we swear in court on Bibles, though perhaps we should swear on fig leaves instead.

This word-history canard wanders about in various forms—here's one I encountered recently: "It was the accepted practice in Babylonia 4,000 years ago that for a month after the wedding, the bride's father would supply his son-in-law with all the mead he could drink. Mead is a honey beer, and because their calendar was lunar based, this period was called the 'honey month' or what we know today as the 'honeymoon.'"

The etymology is fanciful (and even—appropriate to the thought of honeymooning—romantic), but unlikely.[34] The etymology denies two aspects of word creation:

1) Simplicity. Why wouldn't whoever created the word (long after the reign of the Babylonians, considering that these ancients probably didn't speak English) have called it "meadmonth" in direct reference to the mead and not to one of its ingredients?

2) Poetry. Fact is, people have poetry in our souls and our words. The more accepted etymology for this word supposes that *honey* is used figuratively, to refer to the sweetness of that first month of marriage. Also in poetic reference, the month is referred to as moon. And in fact, it's likely that there's dark poetry involved—a cynical implication that the first sweet weeks wane as quickly as the new moon.

Finally, the mead bacchanalia explanation also denies one aspect of human nature: As Word Detective Evan Morris has written, "Why did the bride's father want his new son-in-law dead drunk for the first month of his daughter's marriage?"

---

[34] For some reason, tales espousing the mead-extravaganza explanation embellish it by noting that Attila the Hun supposedly died on his honeymoon night because he was so drunk that he choked to death. Now there's a romantic thought. And one that ignores the fact that Attila had had many honeymoon nights and many drunken sprees before then. He was a barbarian, after all. I can see it now, a bullshitternetymology that Attila was so Hunnie he mooned everyone.

SIRLOIN

File under "Loin, Sir": Some false etymologies do not even deserve discussion that's as long as this very subhead.

The scene: King James I enjoys his beef loin repast so much he beknights it. Yeah. Right.[35]

FIRED!, YOU'RE

Giving the sack to stupid etymologies

Here's a cute Internet-driven myth about a slang phrase that likely rose from the days of mimeographed bulletin-board postings, which in turn likely rose from the "long-ago" days of town criers spouting idiotic folk etymology. Well, the town criers didn't do that, to my knowledge, but for a moment, imagine the clang of bells and shouts of "Hear ye! Hear ye! Clans of long ago that wanted to get rid of their unwanted people without killing them used to burn their houses down—hence the expression, 'to get fired'!" *Clang clang clang.*

So goes one etymological canard, to which I clang my bell and cry in return, "Hear Ye! Hear Ye! Yeah, sure, and Donald Trump was holding the torch, made out of scripts from *The Apprentice* and possibly his toupée!"

Ignore the fact that somewhat barbarous people were unlikely to investigate compromise relocation solutions for their neighbors

---

[35] OK, I never said the footnote had to be shorter than the subhead, so here's more of the story: *Sirloin* came over from Old French as *surloinge*, meaning the cut of meat that was above (*sur*) the loin. You see this prefix in *surpass* ("to go beyond"), *surcharge* ("to charge extra"), *survive* ("to live beyond"), and the long obsolete but too-lovely-to-ignore *sur-clouded* ("shaded from above"). Also—*surname*, the name above the name, or beyond the name. Now, *surname* experienced the same spelling shift as *surloin*—*I* instead of *U*—for a time, because the folk etymology at the time associated the word with one's father, or *sire*. John Williamson is John, William's son, so it would make sense that William's son was the "sir name." But that bit of mistaken punnery didn't take hold, and so the spelling remains *surname*. On the other hand, the punnery around benighting one's meatsteak very likely set the *sirloin* spelling into concrete. By the way, it seems kings ate very well in Medieval times, as one would expect, as joining James I ("the second Solomon") as the purported beknighter in the lands of Etymologia Mythica are Charles II ("the Merrie Monarch") and Henry the VIII ("I am I am").

who irritated them because of who knows why (didn't mow their lawns often enough? played their stereo bagpipes too loud after dusk?). I suspect that such clans relied on that classic relocation solution known as a "threat." *We don't want to kill you, so leave, and we won't.* Saves matches that way.

Now, layer on the fact that "to fire" someone is *American* slang. I challenge the author of this myth to name more than zero "clans of long ago," *Braveheart* style, in the U.S., which doesn't actually have that much "long ago." And a synonym of *fire*, as in "fire a gun," is *discharge*. Which can mean . . . well, it doesn't mean "burn your house down."

LIES IN THE 1500S
As in fibs and fabrications, details in etymologies are often distracting.

In the above entry on the origin of the slang phrase "You're fired," the false history referred to the neighbor-removal tactics of "clans of long ago." The phrase "long ago" is one of those telltale signs of bullshitternetisms, although naming specific places and times doesn't necessarily lead to veracity.

One bullshitternet classic is "Life in the 1500s," recounting such "facts" as: "You've heard of thatched roofs, well that's all they were [thatched grammar, well that's what they had, too]. Thick straw, piled high, with no wood underneath. They were the only place for the little animals to get warm. [By the fire was obviously not an option.] So all the pets; dogs, cats and other small animals, mice, rats, bugs, all lived in the roof. When it rained it became slippery so sometimes the animals would slip and fall off the roof. Thus the saying, 'it's raining cats and dogs.'"

Obviously, animals in the 1500s were much different from those of today. Cats slipped a lot. Dogs were smart enough to figure out that heat rises, which is no surprise because they also figured out how to climb into the roofs of buildings. On the other hand, they seemed to gravitate to the roof during the rainy season, which is warmer than winter—when one would expect that conditions would be considerably more slippery, leading to a more logical "snowing cats and dogs." Besides, why the cats and the dogs? Why didn't it rain mice and rats? Why not a bug deluge?

"Life in the 1500s" contains a number of such "explanations," and I don't have the space here to appropriately laugh at, mock, and generally jeer them. So I'll defer to a fascinating book called *Word Myths: Debunking Linguistic Urban Legends*, by David Wilton. Track it down. He spends seventeen delicious, "Go get 'em David!" pages debunking "Life in the 1500s," including the domesticated-meteorology myth and other myths surrounding such phrases and words as "throw the baby out with the bathwater," "wake," and "dead ringer."

Final thought: consider the grammar in "Life in the 1500s," such as the bizarre misuse of semicolons and commas in the above excerpt. It's the same grammar you find in emails enticing you to send your bank account numbers to "bank officials" overseas in exchange for millions of dollars, euros, pounds, quatloos, or the currency *d'jour*, or to "click here to activate the computer virus that oddly resembles a naked Angelina Jolie." (*Pssst*—those emails aren't true, either.)

DANGERS OF SPEAKING ENGLISH

The Internet is not a reliable source of information (have I mentioned that before?).

But at least it's the source of a good joke now and again. I'm not sure that this is one of them. I'll condense it:

> The final word on nutrition and health has been revealed. Compared to Americans, Brits, and Canadians, people of various nationalities suffer fewer heart attacks: the Japanese eat very little fat; Mexicans eat a lot of fat; the Chinese drink very little red wine; Italians drink a lot of red wine; Germans consume a lot of beer, sausages, and fats; Ukrainians consume a lot of vodka, pierogis, and cabbage rolls. And all suffer fewer heart attacks. Conclusion: Eat and drink what you like. Speaking English is apparently what kills you.

Can't We Even Get Our Own Clichés Right?

"You can quote me as saying I was misquoted."

–Groucho Marx

If you were misquoted, Groucho, you're a member of a club you don't want to belong to because it would have you as a member.

Let's meet some of Groucho's fellows, the ones who said what they didn't say in ways they didn't say it. Yet, we still "remember" the quotes and the clichés in translations and corruptions as outrageous as the Marx Brothers converting the simple voicing of the word *bum* into a parody of the Spirit of '76 in *The Cocoanuts* in a matter of a few screen seconds.

So it's appropriate that Harpo Marx was the one who said "Outside of a dog, a book is man's best friend; inside of a dog, it's too dark to read." You just couldn't hear him, so the quote often goes mistakenly to Groucho.

Here are some other things Groucho didn't say about English, about writing, and about quotations themselves:

CONCISION

I did not have time to write a short entry (or, for that matter, a short introduction to this section), so I wrote a long one, instead (and I didn't say that).

How appropriate that Mark Twain, he of quick wit and 500-page books, once wrote in correspondence, "I did not have time to write you a short letter, so I wrote you a long one instead." The point is excellent. Writing concisely and directly takes concentration, revision, and allowing a little time to elapse so one can return to a draft with a fresh eye and spot wordiness, redundancy, and passive, unnecessary filler. And when Anton Chekhov, the Russian playwright who moon-lighted as a starship navigator on *Star Trek,* began his correspondence with Twain, he wrote, "I did not have time to write you a short letter, so I wrote you a long one instead," which he also did when dropping Abraham Lincoln a letter that Lincoln never opened, perhaps because he needed the envelope for jotting speech notes, but more likely because he was very busy keeping up with his own correspondence. To a friend in Europe, Lincoln wrote, "I did not have time to write you a short letter, so I wrote you a long one instead." (Lincoln also did not have the time to shorten "four score and seven years ago" into "87," but that's another story *and* a classic Bob Newhart routine.) Lincoln was writing his letter to Francois Marie Arouet, who wrote back, "I did not have time to write you a short letter, so I wrote you a long one instead." Or maybe just "ditto." And cc'd Mark Twain. Francois Marie Arouet *did* however find the time to write a short name: We know him by his nom de plume, Voltaire.

Well, by now you've realized that the above paragraph contains a number of factual errors. Voltaire never said "ditto" to Twain, Anton Chekhov never took orders from William Shatner, and none of the famous people so far mentioned originated the clever line about not having time to write a shorter letter.

Samuel Johnson did, of course.

Well, no, he didn't, either. All of the above-mentioned have been credited for the line (all except Shatner, though that may change shortly), and indeed those on our illustrious cast list may have expressed similar drollery at one time or another. But they did not originate it. In a 1657 letter, Blaise Pascal—scientist, philosopher, namer of early computer programs—wrote "Je n'ai fait celle-ci plus longue que parce que je n'ai pas eu le loisir de la faire plus courte." Now, everything I know about French is wrong, too, so for all I know, this very well could be a soufflé recipe. But I believe people when they tell me that it means "I have made this letter longer than usual, only because I have not had the time to make it shorter."

So, one of the great English clichés isn't from an Englishman or an American or a starship pilot, and it's not even originally in English.

GHOTI

Also file this under *F*: George Bernard Shaw probably did not create the spelling *ghoti*.

It's a fish story, of course—a fish that got away from George Bernard Shaw, he of *Pygmalion, Saint Joan,* and *Man and Superman.* Shaw is generally credited with concocting an anti-phonetically pronounced "fish" by taking the *GH* sound from *laugh,* the *O* sound from *women,* and the *TI* sound from *potion.*[36] It's a fun and oft-quoted word fabrication designed to deride quirks in our language, though its point is blunted when you consider that you could spell *fish* this way *only* if the *f*-pronounced *GH* ever ever once started a word in English, *only* if the *sh*-pronounced *TI* ever ever once closed a word in English, and *only* if *O* was ever ever once pronounced as a short *I* in any English word but *women.* (It would also be a sharper barb if *English* were spelled *Engloti.*)

Now, George Bernard Shaw was a vigorous proponent of spelling reform, but first mentions of *ghoti* appear some eight years before linguist Mario Pei hands the catch to Shaw in 1946, and they

---

[36] When responding to the question, "What is 'ghoti'?," writer Jim Scobbie responded, "It's an alternative spelling of *chestnut.*"

appeared with no reference to him. *The Christian Science Monitor,*
on August 27, 1938, wrote "A foreigner who insisted that 'fish'
should be spelled 'ghoti' explained it in this fashion. . . ." Shaw was
British, and thusly qualifies as a foreigner to an American paper,
but likely said paper would have recognized this particular
foreigner. In *Finnegans Wake,* published in 1939, James Joyce
writes: "Gee each owe tea eye smells fish." (Yeah, "smells" fish—
Joyce was a jenius.) And the London *Times* quotes a Dr. Daniel
James delivering the amusing concoction in a speech.

But the most compelling evidence that Shaw did not create this
fish story? The fact that he never followed up by taking the *TI* from
potion and the *OUGH* from *thought* to spell his own last name.

GREEK TO ME, IT'S ALL

Shakespeare did not originate the cliché, "It's all Greek to me."

I would translate the phrase "Graecum est; non potest legi," but it's
all Greek to me.

Actually, it's all Medieval Latin to me and to the rest of the world.
And even though it is Latin, it is still all Greek to me, in rough translation. Literally translated: "It's Greek; it cannot be read."

This phrase predates Shakespeare's use—he's often credited for
the phrase—by a year, give or take a century. Yes, Shakespeare put
these English words into the mouth of Casca (in *Julius Caesar*):
"Those that understood [Cicero] smiled at one another and shook
their heads; but for mine own part, it was Greek to me." Word
expert Michael Quinion points out that even then, Shakespeare
wasn't the first playwright to use it: "But virtually the same phrase
had been used the year before (1600) by another Elizabethan

playwright, Thomas Dekker: 'I'll be sworn he knows not so much as one character of the tongue. Why, then it's Greek to him.'"

The Greeks needn't take all the heat, however. To start wandering around the globe, I've seen Internet forum discussion of this phrase claiming that German idiom blames the Spanish, Argentinian idiom blames the Chinese, and Mexican idiom possibly now blames the English-speakers. The Spanish phrase "hablar en griego"—"to speak in Greek"—has the same meaning. The phrase may be the source of a pejorative word for English-speakers that word-watchers William and Mary Morris say was first applied by Mexicans to the Irish. Say *griego* ("greego") aloud. With the tongue position going from *EE* to *G*, doesn't this sound a lot like *gringo?*[37]

JESUS CHRIST, ENGLISH SPEAKER
Every politician in the United States did not say, "If English was good enough for Jesus Christ, it's good enough for me."

If one wishes to unquestioningly believe in the ignorance and the pomposity of government officials, it's easy to accept that Sonny Bono said "If English was good enough for Jesus Christ, it's good enough for me" in arguing for making English the national language. Or that Stromm[38] Thurmond said it. Or Robert Byrd, or former Texas governor Miriam A. Ferguson or Senator Paul Simon or Joint National Committee on Language head Davis Edwards or an "unattributed representative speaking to Dr. Davis Edwards" or "a Southern U.S. senator" or "an Arkansas congressman" or "the Texas congressman" or "an unnamed congressman" or "proponents of the Official English movement" or . . . [39]

---

[37] *Griego* begetting *gringo* is a far more credible etymology than the tale contending that *gringo* arises from American troops in the Spanish-American War singing a song called "Green Grow the Lilacs" while marching. *Sound off! Green grow! Sound off! The lilacs!*

[38] Or Strommmmmmmmmmmm, during his longer nap.

[39] All found from various sources, including God himself. Well, maybe not. But the bullshit-ternet crowd just might swallow that claim.

Apparently, the Internet urban mythologists have it that all these people proclaimed thusly at one time or another, or maybe all at once in "We Are the Words!" chorus, with Sonny hitting the high notes. (Too bad it's the wrong Paul Simon, or we'd have a nice Broadway-ready musical comedy going here.)

Now, someone really did say or write the sentence in question—and others repeated it—otherwise it couldn't have made it to this page. For all you know, I wrote it. It boils down to—with apologies to "All You Need Is Love"—nothing you can quote that can't be quoth. But it's unlikely that this particular babblisciousness was an intentional elocution by a public figure. Some wag, some comedy writer, some member of the "they" of "they say" fame, some single human being hiding in a basement creating all urban myths, likely for minimum wage; this is its likely origin. Multiple attribution/sources/locations, especially indistinct ones ("proponents") or, on the other hand, really really specific ones—by one report in the case of this quote, a 2000 Summer Olympics programmer (huh?) who was likely a "repeater"—are heavy clues suggesting urban mythology. This doesn't automatically assign quotes of confused multiple authorship to the pens of wags, of course. For instance, all the politicians who did *not* say "If English was good enough for Jesus Christ, it's good enough for me" apparently *did* say "Sorry for writing such a long letter—if I'd had more time, I'd have written a shorter one." Someone actually did say something like that, so stop thinking about this silly quote and (if you haven't already as it appears just a few pages before this) read the entry under "Concision," page 97.

Why am I working so hard to disprove the "good enough" quote? Because I fear the consequences should that guy in the basement start to promulgate a potentially more accurate version. If the attitude of "If Aramaic was good enough for Jesus Christ, it's good enough for me" takes hold, I'm gonna have serious difficulty first translating this book and then following up with *Everything You Know About Aramaic Is Wrong.*

BURNS, ROBERT *AND* STEINBECK, JOHN

The best-phrased words of mice and men gang up on your aft with glee.

John Steinbeck's classic 1937 novelette *Of Mice and Men* takes its name from an eighteenth-century poem: "To A Mouse, On Turning Her Up In Her Nest With The Plough." This preceding classic was written by Robert Burns (an auld acquaintance who should not be forgot, for reasons we'll see in a moment).

Today, many of us know a line of the Burns poem as "The best laid plans of mice and men often go astray," which is close to its original meaning but hardly its original wording. Steinbeck's rephrasing translates a bit of Scots vocabulary into more readily understood English. Burns first wrote: "The best-laid schemes o' mice an' men/ Gang aft agley."

The translation (and the need for same) is understandable, because "gang aft agley" isn't particularly common elocution these days. And the word *schemes,* synonymous with the word *plans* in the Merry Olde Back Then and still so today, has a negative connotation on this side of the pond. Besides, some words from Burns's time exist only if they have a beat and you can dance to them—words like "auld lange syne" on New Year's Eve, thanks to (among others) Guy Lombardo and the guy who's working to catch up to being older than Guy Lombardo, Dick Clark.

But none of the specifica above are[40] truly related to my point that everything you know about "the best-laid plans" is wrong. If I were to concentrate on the shift in the specific words used, I would be engaging in no more than the "bickering brattle" exhibited by the Mouse when the poem's narrator farmer digs up Her Nest while Ploughing. In a quiet moment, I suggest that when we quote "The best laid plans of mice and men often go astray" in either incarnation, we are blunting a mournful, philosophical poem. We usually use the phrase as kind of a poetic "Oops," a learned "That's Murphy's Law for you," an erudite "Shit happens." And in so doing, viewing this line as mere grousing and brattle about present misfortunes, we sap the poem of its regret, its melancholy, its trepidation, as delivered in the final stanza:

> *But, Mousie, thou art no thy lane,*
> *In proving foresight may be vain;*
> *The best-laid schemes o' mice an' men*
> *Gang aft agley,*
> *An' lea'e us nought but grief an' pain,*
> *For promis'd joy!*
>
> *Still thou art blest, compar'd wi' me*
> *The present only toucheth thee:*
> *But, Och! I backward cast my e'e.*
> *On prospects drear!*
> *An' forward, tho' I canna see,*
> *I guess an' fear!*

Regret and melancholy and trepidation—auld acquaintances that are too quickly forgot when we twist Mr. Burns's poem and Mr. Steinbeck's inspired reiteration into a simple "oops."

---

[40] Yes, "none are," as *none* in this case is not intended to be "not one," but negation of a plural group.

THE PROOF IS IN THE PUDDING
No it's not.

"The proof is in the pudding" sounds like some sort of chemical test used by TV-show forensic detectives. "We must test for the presence of *poly-tapioca-morphus,* which will prove the culprit is actually Bill Cosby! Apply the pudding!"

That's one of the problems with clichés, beyond lack of creative thought and simple boring overuse. Some of them, if you stop to think about them, make absolutely no sense.

No, "The proof of the pudding is in the eating." Doesn't matter if it appears delicious, or jiggles firmly when you shake the bowl. The true purpose of the subject in question—in this case, taste and nutrition of the food consumed—is all that ultimately matters. Not that I'm encouraging using such overwrought phrases, but one can actually *freshen* this cliché by returning it to its original phrasing. We're so conditioned to the misuse of this hoary phrase that proper quotation will illuminate and enliven it. In that sense, the proof is in the putting, and the putting is in the reading: putting all the words in, and in the right order.

TWAIN, MARK
Mark Twain is not always accurately quoted (then again, as we're seeing so frequently, who is?).

Mark Twain did not write, "The difference between the right word and the almost right word, is the difference between lightning and a lightning bug," as he has been so often quoted.

Mark Twain was a better writer than that. He wrote: "The difference between the almost right word & the right word is really a large matter—it's the difference between the lightning bug and the lightning."

This is important on two levels.

One, it's a matter of Getting It Right, out of respect not only to one of the masters of the language but also to *everyone*—all of us deserve to be quoted not only for what we said but also for what we meant.

Two, it is indeed a matter of preserving the artistry of Twain's statement.

The misquote diminishes the point when it places lightning first and bug second. The lightning flashes out of context, and then the bug blinks weakly as the thunder disappears. The actual quote builds to thunderous crescendo; it introduces the affable lightning bug and then trumps it mightily with the lightning itself. Punchline. Climax. Apex.

The difference between the almost right quote and the right quote? Indeed, the silent blinking and the thunder.

TIME, AT THIS POINT IN
Clichés aren't always totally boring.

In a previous century, when the Watergate break-in scandal was a hot issue, we discovered that then-President Richard Nixon had secretly recorded White House conversations, and we further discovered that these tapes had a mysterious eighteen-minute gap. This was a "point in history" when the phrase "at this point in time" was heard far far too frequently, especially in testimony in the Congressional hearings that commanded our attention in a way unparalleled until OJ's glove stopped fitting. Not long after, "at this point in time" became a spokescliché of redundancy. As well it should have. Still—let's take another look at it.

Don't get me wrong. "At this point in time" is still idiotic verbosity. But consider it in the light of one early meaning of the word *point*. In a century even more previous, in Medieval times (literally), the English word *point* meant one-fifth of an hour. Twelve minutes. So would that gap in the Nixon Tapes more accurately be "at that point and a half of time"?

DONNE, AND UN-DONNE

"No man is an island" is not the cliché it used to be.

Don't get me wrong, "No man is an island, entire of itself" is solid, effective metaphor, especially when Donne embellishes it with consistent imagery: "every man is a piece of the continent, a part of the main. If a clod be washed away by the sea, Europe is the less, as well as if promontory were, as well as if a manor of thy friend's or of thine own were."

But I submit that an earlier piece of imagery in *Devotions upon Emergent Occasions* might more deeply resonate with writers and word lovers, overlooked imagery that should be revived, especially in the light that "No man is an island" has become one of our indelible clichés.

Consider:

> And when she [the Church] buries a man, that action concerns me: all mankind is of one author and is one volume; when one man dies, one chapter is not torn out of the book, but translated into a better

> language; and every chapter must be so translated. God
> employs several translators; some pieces are translated
> by age, some by sickness, some by war, some by justice;
> but God's hand is in every translation, and his hand
> shall bind up all our scattered leaves again for that
> library where every book shall lie open to one another.

I offer this not as theological perspective, but as an example of
the poetry that fades away when clichés are allowed to rule our
language and our memory of the classics.

CHURCHILL, WINSTON (PART I)

File under "Up or Shut Up, Put (Part I)": Winston Churchill
also is not always quoted accurately.

A fun toy you can find on the Internet is a Shakespearean Insult
Generator, a program that grabs one from column A and one
from data bucket B and one from text field C to come up with
such contumely as "Thou pukey motley-minded baggage!" *Pukey?*
Look it up—damn if it isn't really Shakespearean. *Baggage*, too, by
the way.

I wonder if the creators of such generators worry about ending
their insults with prepositions. I ask because I'd like to see them
write a Churchill Preposition Witticism Generator. Winnie's clever
"that is the sort of nonsense up with which I shall not put" is almost
never quoted correctly, and even the anecdote varies wildly in location, situation, and cast of characters. So, we need a little program
that would randomly select items from the following lists—all variations I found on the bullshitternet and in print and in asking my

neighbor odd Gloria two doors down—to possibly generate the actual quote.

As the story goes . . .

[the speaker]
Churchill

[the action]
wrote
scribbled
sent a memo
said
red-pencilled

[the word TO]
to

[the recipient]
an editor
a reporter
a secretary
a member of parliament
a civil servant
a heckler
a speechwriter
a student

[the first words]
This is

[the variable bombast]
arrant pedantry
the kind of arrant pedantry
the sort of pedantry
a bit of arrant pedantry
the type of errant pedantry
an objection
a proposition
a situation
a practice
a rule
something
insubordination
English
the kind of English
the sort of English
the sort of thing
the kind of thing
one thing
the sort of nonsense
the sort of criticism
the sort of errant criticism
the sort of bloody nonsense
the kind of tedious nonsense
the kind of pedantic nonsense
the kind of offensive
    impertinence
the kind of impertinence

[the operative phrase]
up with which

[the actor]
I
we

[the negative]
will not
shall not
cannot

[the final word]
put

At least in all the examples I found, the *put* stays put.

Spin the wheels on this quotational slot machine a million times, a billion times, perhaps even an infinite number of times, and you won't get an accurate quote, because there are no options for "**[the speaker]**" other than Churchill. It's not likely that he originated the quote, and there's scant evidence that he said it at all, even to repeat it. The quote is likely the work of some wag—and in fact, the first mention of the clever protest against pedantry is recorded in 1942, attributing it to an unnamed "original writer" of a memo in a "certain Government department" in response to a "pedant" who questioned a lonely trailing preposition. Churchill's name isn't added to the story until six years later.

Even winstonchurchill.org calls the tale "apocryphal," and concludes its discussion of the quote by saying, "Verdict: An invented phrase put in Churchill's mouth." Or, "An invented phrase into which Churchill's mouth put."

CHURCHILL, WINSTON (PART II)

File under "Up or Shut Up, Put (Part II)": Some people can't take a joke.

We've all heard the quote, misattributed to Winston Churchill, made in defiance of the "rule" proscribing prepositions, sentences ending in (especially if you just read the entry immediately preceding this one). For the random browsers, that quote goes something along the lines of "This is the sort of bloody nonsense up with which I shall not put." People jumbling that line in so many ways led to the Churchill Preposition Witticism Generator in the entry immediately preceeding this one. And in fact people jumble it so completely that some end up turning it into its opposite. On a website listing famous quotes, I found: "Ending a sentence with a preposition is something up with which I will not put." This version supports the "arrant pedantry" that the non-Churchill was actually railing against. The strange negation is so common that I also found "From now on, ending a sentence with a preposition is some-thing up with which I will not put." I didn't have to look far. It was on *the same page* as the previously quoted version.

But that's OK. Even when people get the quote right, it's a lie. Or at least it's not being true to itself. If the apocryphal jibe were to be written with "arrant pedantry," it would read, simply and unpreten-tiously, "This is the sort of bloody nonsense I shall not put up with." Not very quotable, is it?

"This is the sort of bloody nonsense I shall not put up with" doesn't end with a preposition. *With* is part of the verb phrase "to put up with," synonymous with the infinitive verb *to tolerate*. To clarify, let's examine the sentence, "You put up with me." If you and I were storing Christmas ornaments on the top shelf, you would be putting (the ornaments) up *with* (as in "along with") me, and in this case *with* would be a preposition. But when you the reader put up with me, you are tolerating me, and I am thanking you profusely and moving gently on to the next topic so I don't further test your tolerance with interminable discussion of this topic.

BRITISH VS. AMERICAN ENGLISH

This is the sort of misattribution up with which I shall not put (though that's an entirely different entry—see above).

We see again and again that certain people seem to be quote magnets. They "say" things they've never said. But people associate certain types of profundities and witticisms with specific personalities. In fact, the acknowledgments page of this very book honors a gentleman who has lost bits and pieces of fame because samples of his wit and eloquence have been attributed to his peers.

In this particular entry, we're discussing (for the moment, anyway) the appropriately named Mr. Wilde (first name, Oscar). As Leo Knowles writes on worldwidereference.com, "Oscar Wilde famously declared that Britain and America were two nations divided by a common language. Actually he didn't quite say that but he should have done, which is why he is always misquoted." (I hope I quoted Mr. Knowles correctly. . . .)

For the record, Sir Winston Churchill said "Britain and America are two nations divided by a common language."

No he didn't. But Churchill is another quote magnet (also see our Churchill Preposition Witticism Generator on page 109), and has been credited with the "two nations divided" quip. Actually, Bertrand Russell said it.

No he didn't. He *did* write in 1944 (in *The Saturday Evening Post*): "It is a misfortune for Anglo-American friendship that the two countries are supposed to have a common language." Actually, Dylan Thomas said it.

No he didn't. He did write that we were "up against the barrier of a common language," as published in *The Listener* in 1954. Actually, Oscar Wilde said it. You knew it all along, didn't you?

Except he didn't. Wilde's version in the land of *Great Minds Quip Alike* is from 1887's *The Canterville Ghost*: "We have really everything in common with America nowadays except, of course, language." But it definitely was *not* George Bernard Shaw who said it.

Well, it likely is Shaw, actually, who said "England and America are two countries separated by the same language."[41] And you can quote him on that, because he also has been credited with saying, "I often quote myself. It adds spice to my conversation."

---

[41] Does it ever make you wonder why that quote is never mis-attributed to an American? Or an Australian?

I Am Aware of the Target I'm Placing on My Back

Dammit, I stand upon the grammar mountain and invite lightning bolts from the grammar gods. I am the rod, my arm held high—hit me with the enlightening bolts.

I am here to defend the downtrodden, the outcast, the *hopefully*s and the *ain't*s and the possessive *it's*es and the banished double negative. Even as I write these words I hear persnickitorial screaming; I see anguished persnickitorial faces tighten in fury.

Remember, I warned you I was going to devilishly advocate some thoughts about English. So let me start out by pointing out what even I consider to be egregious . . . if you remember that the first meaning of egregious was "outrageously *good*."

IMPACT, AS VERB

Using *impact* as a verb is not an abomination. It is a celebration.

Perhaps the greatest impact that the word *impact* has had on English-speakers is its role as a focal point for those who believe that the verbing of nouns is some sort of evil. For their rationale, we might turn to the great philosophers, seventeenth-century Thomas Hobbes and sixteenth-century John Calvin, or even to the greater philosophers, Calvin & Hobbes. In the sorely missed comic strip of that name, young Calvin muses to his stuffed-tiger toy Hobbes, "Verbing weirds language."

How delicious is the verbing of an adjective by young Calvin? Perhaps even more delicious than Frank Clune writing in *Roaming round Darling* (1936), "The Poet accused me of verbing a noun, but I soon fixed him. I threatened to noun a verb."

The fact of the matter is that words in English, to use a baseball analogy, are the perfect utility players. They can play most if not all positions, and fill in with talents that other words might lack. The neologistic process of function-conversion is integral to the history, flexibility, and pure power of English.

Still, converting words from their original state generates continual consternation, and in this case, *to impact* has become the ugly standard bearer of a supposedly rapidly deteriorating language.

Well, if we're going to play the reactionary nothing-must-change game, let's set our sights on another less obvious target: the word *impact*. But this time, let's assail it as a noun synonymous with *effect*. For one, if you are to argue that the noun *impact* is not allowed to change, then you are limited to its first meaning, "collision," in use by the late 1700s. Two things can possibly collide without affecting each other. The connotation of "effect" comes a bit later, by the early 1800s. And if we stick with the idea that the first form of the word should not change, then . . . well, the verb came first. Granted, not in the meaning we use it in today: *to impact* by the early 1600s was to "pack in," kind of like what I do with my numerous garbage bags into my one garbage can every Tuesday evening. The lighting-rod meaning was first recorded in 1935.

Now, specific to current use of *impact* as a verb, I myself shall play lightning rod, proclaiming: "Not only is impact perfectly acceptable in verb usage, it is *perfect* in verb usage."

Why? For one, *to impact* has no precise synonym. Its unique connotation carries the seemingly self-contradictory virtues of nuance and power that its oft-nominated replacement, *affect*, does not. A 5-cent-a-gallon hike in gas prices affects you. A dollar-a-gallon hike in gas prices impacts you.

But the other beauty of the word is its marriage of form and content. The price hike will *immmmmmmm-PACT!* you. It's like a bomb dropping. You hear the silence, then the hum, and then the plosives. *To impact* exhibits near-onomatopoeic poetry.

And it does so while serving both function and language convention. People don't create or convert words just to irritate the persnickitors (well, people other than me, anyway)—they do it because the words do work that no other words do. Verbing is not bad English. *To impact* is not a bad infinitive.

In fact, you might say that converting *impact* into a verb is a matter of Englishing the word *impact*. And if you can verb a word like *English* (first recorded use, the '80s—the 1380s, that is), why can't you verb other words?

So, persnickitors, does my bold claim affect your sensibilities? Or does it impact them?

HOPEFULLY

You should not feel sorry for someone who busts a forehead vein over the word *hopefully;* he or she is so anal-retentive as to deserve it.

The word that arguably attracts most persnickitors' attention and usually ire is *hopefully*, as in, "Hopefully you're still awake after reading this." When I write that quoted material, I mean to communicate that "I am hopeful that you're still awake," as opposed to "With hope in your ever-lovin' heart, you are still awake."

But, if those same persnickitors were to read the first ten words of the above paragraph, would they have decried the floating adverb *arguably?* Or *usually?* Interestingly, they probably would not. So, perhaps they will allow *hopefully* to step in line with other such accepted siblings as *arguably, luckily, curiously, fortunately, coinciden-tally* . . . and *interestingly* . . . and, finally, *finally*.

AIN'T

Ain't am not bad English.

In fact, *ain't* is quite good English. It's just not generally accepted English.

Let's look at how the word is constructed. "I ain't" is a contraction of "I am not." It avoids the clumsy contraction "amn't" (which makes a pretty good onomatopoeic representation of a lumpy gulp). And it follows the construction of words like "won't" and "shan't," in which ending consonants are swallowed (maybe in that big lumpy gulp). *Ain't* exhibits a change of vowel pronunciation just like *won't,* which actually features a change of the vowel itself.

I submit that that very vowel change may have led in part to the disdain for *ain't* (should we call that "disdain't"?). In "I ain't," the pair of shrill long vowels in combination—*aye ay*—grates the ear, and sends the speaker's tongue into a bit of gymnastics. Would the word be more acceptable if the *A* were to retain its short-*A* pronunciation, as in "I an't"? Perhaps, although we suddenly have another *ant/aunt* homonym. As well, saying "I an't" perpetuates the voicing of double vowels, whereas the alternate contraction, "I'm not," absorbs one of the vowels and allows easy flow from vowel to consonant. "I an't" is simply more difficult to mouth, a problem that, say, converting "I can not" to "I can't" doesn't face.

Interestingly, my "suggestions" above trace the actual evolution of *I am* to *I amn't* to *I an't* to *I ain't*. How did we get to the sharp-syllabled *ain't?* Sounds a bit strange, perhaps, until you consider another colloquial pronunciation: I cain't.

Again, it's a matter of word fashions, the reason *reckon* sounds backwoods to Americans even though it's very much frontwoods to the Brits.

If you use this perfectly respectable English word *ain't,* use it boldly. It ain't for the fain't of heart.

ITS/IT'S
It's gets it's due.

I shout into the darkness: There is nothing intrinsically wrong with this sentence: "You can't judge a book by it's cover."

I await the persnickitor's nasty missive, writing: "That's an illiterate's statement! It's its! No apostrophe! It's its!"

If that's an absolute, then why would the persnickitor not blink at writing "illiterate's statement" instead of "illiterates statement"? Let's look at it's a bit's more closely.

- "The dog destroyed its master's table legs." Good grammar. Bad dog.
- "The dog destroyed it's masters table legs." Bad grammar. Still bad dog.
- "The dog destroyed it's master's table legs." Bad grammar. Maybe master should get a cat.

Or, in the case of that last sentence, I should say: Good grammar. Bad convention.

Which is my ultimate point. Removing the apostrophe from it's to distinguish possessive from contraction of "it is" or "it has" is convention, and a relatively recent one. Grammatically, you form a possessive by adding apostrophe-s. "It" possesses something. It+apostrophe+s. Yes, it is a pronoun, and no definite pronouns take apostrophes, but its is a recent invention without the pedigree of a his or a hers or a yours.

When the possessive of the ungendered pronoun *it* was first used, it was not its; it was. . . his. He, his; she, hers; it, his. But around 1600, *his* began being replaced with other forms, including *hit* (presumably on the pattern of beginning his and hers with the letter H) and *it's* (constructed the way we construct possessives in general). Shakespeare used both *his* and *it's* as neuter pronoun possessive. But during the 1600s, the spelling of *its* came into play, again presumably on the pattern of other pronoun possessives (mine, his, hers, thine, theirs) sporting no apostrophe, though Evan Morris writes on www.word-detective.com that the waning use of the contraction *'tis* and the confusion caused by its (yes, I know, ironic) replacement it's fueled the rise of *its.*

If *its* is good grammar as a possessive, then why aren't we writing that middle sentence "The dog destroyed its masters table legs"? Why remove one apostrophe and not the other? Perhaps a more pertinent question is Why insert the apostrophe in either? English writers didn't used to. One method of indicating possessives from Old English was adding S—as in *cyninges* (what we would write as *king's*, with the E fully pronounced. But among many changes over time, the vowel was swallowed in speech, and often replaced in writing with an apostrophe indicating the swallowed letter. This is the same mechanism that led to the way swallow'd and other past-tense verbs were often written for a time. But where the apostrophe clung to the writing of possessives, it did not cling to the writing of past tense. Feel edify'd yet?

Any way you look at it, I will continue to use *its*, of course, as the accepted usage as a possessive. But I do so knowing that I'm adhering to convention, usage, and changing language, and not to grammar.

'Tis a darn shame.

OVEREXAGGERATION

File under "Exaggeration, Playing the Over/Under": Let's not overstate the power of overoverstatement.

"*Overexaggeration* is redundant!," the persnickitors cry. (They always use exclamation points.) Not necessarily. *Overexaggeration* might simply be guilty of hyperbole.

To exaggerate is to overstate. Now. One early meaning of *exaggerate* was simply "to pile up"; the meaning of "pile up *too much*" came shortly afterward. And now, to those claiming that *overexaggerate* is to over-redundate (I know, not a word, but it should be), and that the word really means "overoverstate":

To exaggerate is to overstate for effect. To overexaggerate is to take the overstatement a step or more too far—to, potentially, take an exaggeration past the point of legitimate and reasonable overstatement to make a point. If I say that I receive a truckload of junk mail each week, I am exaggerating. If I say that this morning I received every piece of junk mail ever created, and the delivery just crushed my car, I'm overexaggerating. Here's another case where using the word *overex* . . . well, I'm not going to use the word again, because one more reference to this unusual word would likely crush my other car.

ANOTHER

"And a nother thing" is not necessarily bad grammar.

This is a whole nother topic: *Nother* is regarded as a slang corruption of *another*, which of course arises from joining "an other." For example, here's a pretty corrupt use, from a '70s pop song, I think: "a nother lady proud and new." Well, maybe not a '70s tune—I suspect that Chaucer didn't write much pop music in the 1370s. *Nother* was fairly common in Middle English, and resulted from the same sort of mis-split that gave us *an apple* instead of the original *"a napple."*

I find it amusing that *napple* has resurfaced, both as an unrelated slang term (an apple-sized nipple) and, more pertinent to this discussion, as an argument ("Pronouncing 'a napple' is lazy American speech!"). What goes around comes around, or as they used to say, "A-nother day shal torne vs alle to ioie,"[42] also from one of Chaucer's nonpop songs—specifically, *Troilus and Criseyde.*

So between "an other" and "a nother," which is incorrect? *Nother. Nother,* which is a whole nother word literally and figuratively—an obsolete Old English word meaning "neither."

DOUBLE NEGATIVES

File under "No! No! A thousand times no!": Double negatives are not no bad English.

---

[42] Which doesn't really mean "what goes around comes around," but close enough.

When I ask people, "Do you use double negatives?" (just a hint, for all the guys reading this—that's a *terrible* pickup line), they often reply, "No, I don't."

Of course, the single negative "No" would have sufficed, as would the single negative "I don't." But those three words harbor two negatives, perhaps for conversational flow, but more likely for emphasis. And it is within emphasis that the double negative holds its power. Even so, many English speakers would simultaneously agree with, and fail to note the irony of, the sentence, "In English, double negatives are a no-no."

Why such disdain for the double-ought? The Bishop Robert Lowth, in 1762's *A Short Introduction to English Grammar with Critical Notes* (also see page 139), is said to have proscribed: "Two negatives in English destroy one another or are equivalent to an affirmative." Leave it to the good Bishop to ignore the linguistic sibling of the moralistic cliché, Two wrongs don't make a right. Negative-negative destruction? Is the Bishop's evaluation akin to acid/basic chemical reactions? And if negatives destroy each other, perhaps science fiction writers should stop predicting matter-antimatter propulsion systems and instead just throw a bunch of *nots* into a big thruster system. What Bishop Lowth almost certainly meant is that two negatives negate each other, but even then, negation leaves behind not affirmation, but neutrality. Granted, I'm not arguing linguistically here, but then again, neither was the good Bishop.

The Bishop's conclusion implies that by saying "I don't want no apples," I might communicate, "I want apples." Did anyone out there come away believing that that was my intent? Besides, if you apply that level of microparsing to a double-negative sentence, you could equally microparse the "acceptable" alternative: "I don't want any apples." OK, microparsers and persnickitors: Did I mean "I want no apples"? Or did I mean, "I don't want *any* apples—I want Granny Smiths"?

Double negatives are not no bad English—Chaucer used double and even triple negatives. Double negatives are now *nonstandard* English, yes, and if your goal is to be understood and to avoid becoming a linguistic lightning rod, I do not not proscribe their use.

Penultimate thought on this topic: Why is there not a mirror proscription of double positives? Would "Yes, I do" mean "No"? Of course not. On the other hand, listen a moment to Steven Pinker in his *How the Mind Works*: "Philosophers relish the true story of the theoretician who announced at a scholarly conference that while some languages use a double negative to convey a positive, no language uses a double affirmative to convey a negative. A philosopher standing at the back of the hall shouted in a singsong, 'Yeah, yeah.'"

Ultimate thought on this topic: Yes, we have no bananas, we have no bananas today.

EATS
You can't have your eats and cake it, too.

The most popular punctuation book perhaps ever is Lynne Truss's *Eats, Shoots and Leaves*. The title is based on the dangers of comma misplacement. A panda bear who "eats shoots and leaves" is one that is being a proper herbivore, while one that "eats, shoots and leaves" consumes his dinner, fires a sidearm, and absquatulates promptly.

I propose, however, that the comma version can communicate much the same thought that the uncomma version does, if you read *eats* as a noun instead of a verb. What's on the panda's menu?

Eats, shoots and leaves. In other words: food, shoots and leaves. In that light, our cuddly panda remains the proper herbivore, if not the speaker of proper English.

Though it sounds like recent slang corruption along the lines of "Gotta get me a pack of smokes," using *eat* and *eats* as nouns is not a corruption, is not slang, and is not recent, unless, of course, you personally remember the good old days of Old English.

TEACH/LEARN

File under "Learning, a Little": Teaching can not be learned, and learning can not be teached (or taught, for that matter).

Would it jar you if I learned you that *learn* has been used as a transitive verb since the 1300s? And if I then learned you that it was for a long time considered proper English? I learned that from my seventh-grade teach.

UTILIZE

File under "Utile, the Futile": *Utilize* is not a bad word.

The language guard dogs (I among them), so voracious and verbacious (as my colleague Richard Lederer would call them), snapping at and tearing apart verbal flab, flabbery, and flabaciousness, regularly warn against using a long word when a shorter synonym will suffice [**editor's note—why doesn't Brohaugh just say "when a shorter synonym will DO"?**]. For a time, the poster child of flabaciousness seemed to be *utilize,* as in "I utilized my cell phone to call my grandmother."[43] Much shorter (and more appropriately

---

[43] I can hear Grandma saying, "Oh really? When? I don't remember that call."

invisible), is the word *use*, as in "I used the phone to call my grand-mother." (Better yet, how about "I phoned my grandmother"?—though that's a wholly different discussion.)

In this case my fellow guard dogs are correct. But some of the sharp-toothed bunch, still slathering and seething persnickitorially, will next descend on such sentences as "I utilized my cell phone to prop open my eyelids" (probably with Grandma still chattering on the other side). In that sentence, replacing *utilized* with *used* would have been shorter . . . and weaker. In this context, *use* isn't incorrect, but it's also less precise. To utilize something is to make it useful (or, more precisely, to make it *utile*, to employ a now-quite-rare adjective meaning "having utility"). And to utilize something is also to give it a new, undesigned use. For instance, if I pick my teeth with a leather punch (it happened only once, I assure you), I am utilizing the leather punch, not merely using it. I use toothpicks to pick my teeth (well, I do now, anyway).

The point here is that some poster children of flabasciousness and other sins against the language are mere innocent victims with a proper place in speech. In this specific instance, the word *utilize* has both use and utility, and the word *use* has both utility and use. In the larger context of the language: Every word has its utility. Every word has its use.

Mistakes

In his book *Fine Print: Reflections on the Writing Art,* columnist James J. Kilpatrick decried what was literally and figuratively a *bona fide* misuse: Kilpatrick expressed his dismay regarding writers who had spelled the phrase as *bonified* and as *bonafied,* as if one could bonify something—make it real (what was it before?). And therefore the object in question would now be bonified.

Bonified is clearly a mistake. But I would wager, with all due respect to the learned Mr. Kilpatrick, that he himself repeats English mistakes daily. And I can pretty much guarantee that you, my equally esteemed reader, do not go a day without promulgating one or more English goofs. You and I and Mr. Kilpatrick simply accept them these days.

As examples:

You've certainly eaten *an apple.* Oops. The doctors that are being kept away each day will be proud of you, but deep down the linguists should be appalled. You are repeating that common language "mistake," because what you are really eating is *a napple.* But somewhere along the line, we mistake-ridden folk started confusing ourselves about where the *N* went, and darnit if we didn't go and bonify the word *apple.* By mistake.

Do you have *a nickname?* Oops. (And eek, to boot.) You have *an eke name* (*eke* meaning "extra"), swallowed and reseparated into *a nickname.* And so it is with the other words we no longer use by mistake, including *napron, nadder, numpire* and *nauger* on one side of the wandering *N,* and *otch* and *ewt*[44] on the other side.

These are cases of "metanalysis," a technical coinage from 1914 describing "reanalyzing" word patterns. That's very kind. They're mistakes.

---

[44] "He turned me into a newt," said the ewt in *Monty Python and the Verbal Grail.* But he's getting better.

Other mistakes over the centuries result from various types of speech patterns and repatterns and, yes, even reanalyzing. You've eaten a caper before, yes? Here I would say oops, but since this is a single mistake, I will say oop. *Capers* came to English as one of those words both singular and plural, but we depluralized it by removing the *S*. So it was with *pea* (see page 148 for more on that) and, in a sense, *cherry*. Oop.

And then there's pure "folk etymology," where people change syllables and sometimes entire words to syllables and words more common in their lives. A *chaise lounge* chair is a corruption of the original French *chaise longue* (literally, "chair long"); *cherry* is a corruption of French *cherise*, misinterpreted as a plural; *shamefaced* puts a blushing human face into the original *shamefast;* and so on. Each of these mistakes and corruptions have become bona fide.

What's more, I say with more conviction than alarm, they will become bonified, as well.

Now let's take a look at a few other words that have mistakenly earned their bonafides.

COULD

File under "Woulda Couda Shoulda": The Little Engine That Could, couldn't.

Could it be true that English is composed of so many now-accepted mistakes? Could be, and is. Ever use the word *could?*

The past indicative tense of the verb *can* used to be spelled *coud,* but because the word rhymed with the past indicatives of *will* and *shall—would* and *should—*people began slipping the *L* into *coud* by analogy. Why do we make such "mistakes"? Because we can. And why did we make that particular mistake? Because we coud.

THE BIG CHEESE

The slang phrase "The big cheese" will not trigger lactose intolerance.

"The big cheese" and "the high muckamuck" are roughly synonymous phrases, one, of course, with American origins and referring to food, and the other of foreign heritage, with no specific relation to food. Both slangishly mean the bigwig, the grand poobah, the head honcho, the person in charge.

What's my point? Everything you know about English is wrong, of course. The American food-related phrase is "high muckamuck," Anglicizing the Chinook native American phrase *hiu mucka-muck,* meaning "plenty of food." Someone who had plenty of food back in the very early 1900s when the phrase was first recorded apparently was pretty well off.

The big cheese, on the other hand, almost certainly comes from a Persian or Urdu word meaning "thing": *chiz.* It's said that in the early 1800s, Anglo-Indians slangishly "translated" the phrase "the real thing" into "the real chiz," which, by homonymic association, came to be spelled the same way as our curdy *mucka-muck.* The word wandered across the pond to America, where it came to mean first wealth and then the one with the wealth (and likely plenty of food, too) in the early 1900s.

So any etymology claiming that the original big cheeses were those monstrous cheese wheels is a "Swiss cheese etymology"—full of holes.

HANGNAIL

You don't have the definition of *hangnail* nailed.

Years ago I suffered a plantar wart (and not a planter's wart—see page 9) in the sole of my foot. This "wart," actually a viral infection imbedded in my tender tootsie skin, hurt like hell. Hurt like a nail driven up through the bottom of my foot. This is not an imagined comparison, given that when I was in the first grade, I stepped on a spike lingering below the surface of a "muddy" barnyard, the spike driving itself up through my foot between bone and cartilage and tenting the skin on the top of my foot by an inch. This led to hospitalization, big bandages, and lots of cool coloring-book presents from my aunts and uncles. So, yes, hurt like a nail driven through my foot. Hurt like a hangnail.

A hangnail?

The nail-powerful pain of that owie irritating one of your fingers, that little bit of tender flesh that somehow got torn away from the area around your fingernail? How do we compare that quickly healed annoyance to a spike being driven up through your foot, leading to great coloring books?

I grant you, I've never gotten any cool toys for having a hangnail in the word's modern sense, as I apparently secured all possible loot from experiencing the physical version of the word's original sense.

The *nail* in *hangnail* meant—figuratively—the iron type (the kind I stepped on). An *angnægl* was, in Old English, compressed flesh within flesh, figuratively a nail in flesh (a corn, for instance, or, yes, a plantar wart). Likely over the centuries, one syllable changed in meaning by folk etymology from iron nail to fingernail or toenail, while the other changed in both spelling and meaning from *ang-* to *ag-* to *hang-*, bringing us to the present meaning of flesh that hangs near the nail, as opposed to nail that pierces the flesh.

And here I am today, still involved in coloring books—but this time I'm writing them. Pass me the burnt umber crayon; I have another entry to write.

ISLE/ISLAND

File under "I'll, Aisle, Isle"—and fisle it, too: Isles are not islands.

In my radio-writing subcareer, I had opportunity to script a series of commercials for a nationally syndicated radio commentator—or at least one of his characters. The series told the story of this character's endorsement of his local convenience store. In one episode, he talks about the helpful staff, and to demonstrate, he asks a stockboy where the bread is.

"Aisle 2," says the cheery, helpful stockboy.
"OK, how about the beef jerky?"
"Aisle 4."
"And where do you keep the girly magazines?"
"Aisle kill you!" screams his wife, who, unbeknownst to our hero, has happened upon the scene.

I tell this story so I can point out that despite the homonym, *aisle* and the contraction *I'll* have nothing to do with each other, which in turn allows me to segue (radio term, that) to the obvious fact that neither have relationship to homonymous *isle,* which in turn allows me to segue to a discussion of how *isle* and *island* are related.

They aren't.

Isle is not a contraction of *island,* and the two words came to English through entirely different routes.

Oh, they are synonyms, but they are etymologically unrelated. And I grant you that two authoritative bits of evidence would seem to confirm solid relationship. One, of course, is the spelling similarity. But the far more compelling bit of evidence comes from no less of a language authority than the team of songwriter George Wyle and TV producer Sherwood Schwarz, who collaborated on "The Ballad of Gilligan's Island." This poignant mini-opera concludes with the haunting words, "here on Gilligan's Isle," despite Wyle and Schwarz's probable understanding of the full name of the show. This has probably confounded deconstructionist music and language experts for years.

Island traces back to Old English, and one of its original senses denoted a piece of land bordered by a lot of water, and referred to peninsular territory or high ground that became isolated during flooding. Early spellings of *island* include *igland, iland, illond, yllond,* and *ile-land.* But then this Old French word *isle* came along by around the year 1300. *Isle* traces back to the Latin *insula,* meaning "island" (the Professor would certainly understand that the castaways were *insulated*).

Ironically, *isle* had lost its *S* by the time it was brought into Middle English as *ile,* but during the Renaissance learned Latin orthographers in France apparently thought that restoring the noble *S* was the pointy-headed thing to do, and apparently the English followed suit. *Ile* reabsorbed the *S,* and eventually, so did English *iland* because of association with French *isle. Island* had established itself as the accepted spelling by the beginning of the eighteenth century. Meanwhile, what's the modern French word meaning "island"? Of course, simply *île.*

And in a different sort of irony, the word *aisle* that I so shockingly revealed to you was unrelated to *isle* shared some orthographic history with the word—it, too, had no *S* in it, until "learned" Middle French orthographers decided it needed to be Latinized. (Next, we'll have to figure out where to insert a silent *S* into the contraction *I'll. Is'll? I'sll?* Hmm.)

In the cases of the former *aile, ile,* and *iland,* who blundered and dropped that silly extra *S* in? I'll blame Gilligan!

BLINDFOLD

There are no folds in a blindfold. No blinds, either, but that's a decorating matter and not word-history matter.

Have you ever noticed that there are no crisp creases in a blind-fold, no pleats, no folds? If you say that you never looked or even thought about it, I will accept that answer (though the suspicious part of me will wonder if you didn't notice because you were wearing a blindfold at the time and I'm not sure that I want to hear about your blindfold-wearing adventures and whether you were offered that last cigarette before the firing squad was called to attention, or whether you were offered that cigarette after that delightful evening with your loved one last weekend . . .).

If you respond, "You know, you're right," I won't inquire further (because you obviously were on the other side of the blindfold, and either still holding the gun, or offering the cigarette to your loved one last weekend . . .).

Anyway, as I step cautiously, carefully, delicately out of firing range, I will point out that if you've assumed that the *fold* relates to the cloth of a blindfold, it's because you were *blind-felled,* struck blind, by that familiar word *fold.* Rather, you were deceived, as the *fold* is a variation of *felled.* You were *blind-struck,* which is a word that

I'm glad no one used, because if *blind-felled* became *blindfold*, there's a chance that *blind-struck* might have morphed into *blind-sock*, which is just too odd an image to consider.

BUTTONHOLE

File under "I'll Order One Shirt, Hold the Buttons": There is no hole in buttonhole (to begin with, anyway).

Buttonhole has nothing in common with *buttonhold*, the word we folk-etymologized to create *buttonhole*. The original *buttonhold* was a loop of string put round the button so to keep one's shirt on. The progression from *buttonhold* to *buttonhole* is hardly a leap of physical or semantic logic, so why do I say that the words have nothing in common? Well, what's in the middle of each? *Nothing*. And that's what they have in common. Until they fasten the button, that is.

MANO A MANO

You don't have to be a male to go mano a mano—in fact, you don't even have to be human.

The phrase "mano a mano" is, of course, not English at all. It's Spanish, and its adoption by faddish catch-phrasers, particularly before the turn of the millennium, demonstrates a danger of borrowing foreign phrases into a language. For those who understand that "I'll confront him mano a mano" does *not* mean "I'll confront him man to man," I give you a big hand. Or even a regular hand, whatever you like, and then you and I can go mano a mano.

In Spanish, *mano* means "hand." *Mano a mano* means "hand to hand," as in a style of combat engaged in primarily by males, but certainly not necessarily so. The word traces back to Latin *manus*, "hand."

On the other mano, if *mano a mano* were to be accepted by most English speakers as meaning "man to man," then that's what it means. Why shouldn't *mano a mano* join other now-acceptable English words that attribute their meanings to mistaken foreign borrowings (for example, *cherry*, page 149; *crayfish*, page 136; *alligator*, page 30)?

In a sense, we might say that we have been *manipulated* (worked by hand, not by man) into a *manufactured* (made by hand, not by man) English meaning.

REPLENISH
File under "Plenish, Re-": *Replenish* was originally not a synonym of *resupply*.

Why can you replenish something but not plenish it in the first place? Because there is no sense of "again" or of repetition in the original meaning of the word *replenish*. That word came to English in the 1300s from Old French *repleniss-*, and it simply meant "to stock" or "to fill up" (in fact, *replenished*—indicating "full"—arrived before the verb *replenish* did). But mistaking the *re-* as the prefix meaning "again," we began by the early 1600s to use the word to mean "restock."

You'd think that that change in meaning would leave a void that would have to be, um, replenished, and that back-forming *plenish* might fill the bill of lading. And the word *plenish* was indeed used, though briefly and rarely and not in reaction to the shift in the word *replenish*. Ultimately, I suppose that the variety of *plenish* synonyms like *stock* and *supply* made the void left by *replenish* pre-replenished.

MISTLETOE

Even though there's no *toe* in *mistletoe*, you can nonetheless stub your mistletoe.

There are no toes involved with mistletoe, unless, of course, the Christmasy couple are playing footsy while smooching under the mistle twig. *Mistle* is an Old English word describing what we now call mistletoe. By complete mistake. (And by complete *now-accepted* mistake regarding plurals, I remind those who gripe about *kudo*, for reasons explored on page 148.) A *tan* in Old English was a "twig." *Mistletan*, therefore, was a compound meaning a twig of the mistle plant. Now, at that time, plurals were formed with a suffix formation that we'll punningly call "N-dings." One ox, two oxen. One brother, two brethren. *Tan* was also the plural of *ta*, or "toe." So our ancient English speakers looked at *mistletwig* and saw *mistletoes*, and shaved off the *N* pluralization to make the word "singular." A kudo to them.

So how do we stub a mistletoe? Remove the toe entirely, because the "stubbed" *mistle* could perform its old duties more efficiently than the longer *mistletoe*, though our footsy-playing lovers might regret a shorter kiss.

CRAYFISH

A crayfish is neither etymologically nor biologically a fish.

Once when my youngest son was five years old, the two of us were exploring the creek that ran behind our house. Kevin spotted some quick movement in the waters, and pointed. "That's a crawdad," I explained, using the colloquial word for *crayfish*, since it kinda seemed like a colloquial sort of father-son moment.

Kevin watched the "crawdad" a bit until we colloquially began splashing about a bit, skipped some rocks, rested on the bank. A few quiet minutes later, Kevin shot a pointy-finger at movement near the edge of a small sandbar. "Look! Crawldad!"

Overcome by cute, I didn't explain to him that there is no *crawl* in *crawdad*. Nor did I explain (to him or to myself) that there's also no *craw*, and certainly no *dad*, in *crawdad* or *crawfish* (as it's often called in the States)[45], just as there's no *fish* in *crawfish/crayfish*. All those syllables are mistakes—understandable mistakes, but mistakes nonetheless.

Based purely on appearances (both of the word and of the creature itself), the analogy of *crayfish* to *fish* could be understandable. Watery denizens might be termed fish in aggregate, the way the word *deer* once referred to all animals. But that's not in any form the case. As I said, it's all a mistake.

The word for one of the smallest of crustaceans crawldadded over the English channel from Old France (where they spoke Old French, though they didn't consider it "old" at the time) as *crevice*, and was adapted into Middle English with a couple of spellings, including *crevisse*. Two points to consider about *crevisse*: one, it was originally accented on the second syllable as it was in Old French, which led to variant English pronunciations of the first syllable, including a broadened pronunciation of the long-*A* sound into "craw." Two, *visse* was confused with the Middle English word *vish* or *viss*—"fish"—confusion that led to the modern spelling of the word *crayfish*.

So where does *dad* come into the story? I'm Kevin's Dad, of course.[46]

---

[45] I love this quote found in a web forum, attributed to Herb Stahlke: "I ate crawdads, not crawfish, when I lived in Georgia. Anything else would stick in the cray."

[46] For the "dad" discussion, let me turn the lectern over to *The Natchez Naturalist Newsletter*: " . . . it seems to arise from the general impulse among Southern country people to be colorful and folksy with their language. Maybe it has something to do with what the crawdad looks like when he's in his burrow looking up at you with his claws ready, like a grumpy old man at his front door." What did I tell you? The *dad* in *crawdad* is grumpy me.

DORD
D is not for Ddictionary

It's not a word you use every day, because it's not a word anyone used at all, yet it appeared in the dictionary. There are a few of these "ghost" words, including *dord*. This "word," defined as "density," apparently constituted the "New" in 1934's *Webster's New International Dictionary*. (Readers, insert your own "density of editor" joke here.) What happened? *Density* was supposed to be added to a list of words that could be abbreviated as "*D* or *d*." Somehow, the spaces in "*D* or *d*" were lost, and *Dord* was interpreted as a full word. What's most amusing is that some editor inserted the word's pronunciation, even though it had never been pronounced.

There have been other ghost words in dictionaries—a famous one being *esquivalience,* intentionally placed as a copyright trap in the *New Oxford American Dictionary* (the way some mapmakers insert fake streets onto their maps and mailing-list brokers insert the names of fake people into their lists to detect people who steal their hard work).

My favorite part of the unintentional *Dord* story comes in its retelling. You gotta love the little jibe that the myth-busting website Snopes.com added to its coverage of this subject. Run your cursor over the facsimile of the printed error that Snopes includes on the page, and an "alt" window pops up, reading simply: "D('oh)rd!"

You Don't Speak Latin, and Not a Whole Lot of Greek, Either

You do not speak Latin. I suspect that your lack of daily conversance with a dead language does not come as any sort of surprise to you. What may surprise you is that, as an English-speaker, you probably have been chided more than once for speaking improper Latin even though you don't speak it.

What's that all about?

Read on.

ENDING A SENTENCE WITH A PREPOSITION

File under "Prepositions, with Which to Not End a Sen-tence With": We answer the question posed in this section's introduction.

So, once more, what's that all about?

It's about the fact that persnickitors are shuddering at the sentence directly above, the sentence that used the word *about,* a preposition, to end the sentence with. (And they're shuddering at the preposition *with* in the previous sentence, too.) When Bishop Robert Lowth published 1762's *A Short Introduction to English Grammar* (we'd all be better off had it been even shorter), he based several of his principles on a language of the classics, the revered Latin. If a rule applies to Latin, was his thinking, it must be good. With reverence to the classical language, therefore, I should have written not "What's that all about?" but instead "About which is that all?" (which is arguably a Latin sentence, because it sure isn't English—not natural English, anyway, and certainly not communicative English.)

The rule may have lingered in an effort to guard against weak line endings in poetry. For example, when I wrote above "to end the sentence with," the problem was not the position of the preposition, but its very existence. Just cut it for concision, and the sentence makes perfect sense. On the other hand, the poets worried about weak line endings never imagined the Beatles unweakly belting out "Work it on out!" in "Twist and Shout." 'Nuff said.

So, if someone fusses at you for ending a sentence with a preposition (or, as Master Yoda would say, "for sentence ending preposition with"), just reply, "Vos operor non narro Latin" ("You do not speak Latin"). Or better yet, "Quisnam blandior?" ("Who cares?")

SPLIT INFINITIVES

File under "Here's a Big Surprise": Latin has nothing to do with bowling.

When I think of English grammar, I think of standing on Lane 5 of the local Bowl-a-Rama, contemplating the difficulty of converting that challenging spare taunting me at lane's end.

Well, I don't really, because English grammar has nothing to do with bowling. So instead, when I think of English grammar, I think of sitting at my keyboard, fingers poised over the home keys, wearing the same ridiculously striped shoes, and contemplating the difficulty of converting that challenging dead Latin language taunting me at grammar's end.

Well, I don't really do that, either, because as I contend in various places in this book, English *grammar*, unlike English *vocabulary*, has nothing to do with Latin. Which oddly brings us back to bowling.

Consider bowling's two-ten split, not the hardest pin position to rescue a spare from, but a difficult one nonetheless. If you face a two-ten split, you hope that the ball that left you in that position had managed only to *tentatively* split those pins.

Oops! Beware! We disturbed the sacred tomb! All ancient Roman linguists are rising from their graves to keen about how English has corrupted the rules of the language that's as dead as they are. And the English persnickitors who equally have no lives are joining the decaying Roman linguists. And we hear the wails:

First, *"You split an infinitive when you wrote 'to tentatively split' . . ."*

And then: *"Latin rules must govern English! Latin rules must govern bowling!"*

Now, seriously, do either of the statements in the paragraph above make any sense to you? They shouldn't, because they are both equally nonsensical and unsupportable.

I'm engaging in non sequitur punnery, of course, when I write of "two-ten split" and "to tentatively split." . . . You see, the phrase "to tentatively split" egregiously violates Renaissance worship of Latin that has hence dictated that one must not separate the elements of a verb infinitive: the two-pin ("to") from the ten-pin (the following verb). The reality is that this rule is based on Latin word construction, where infinitives are single words. To split a Latin infinitive, therefore, you'd have to take a chisel to it, or whatever tool you would use for cleaving Roman writings. That's akin to saying that because bowling developed from a game called nine-pins, the two-ten split should be officially banned because that classic game didn't have a ten-pin.

So, bowlers and writers alike, have at. You are allowed to skillfully convert the two-ten split.

SPLIT INFINITIVES, PART II[47] . . . ER, PART 2

File under "To Split an Infinitive, Redux[48] . . . er, Revisited" (or "Two Split an Infinitive"): Shakespeare did not write "To be or to not be," but he could have.

We've seen in the entry directly above that splitting an infinitive violates no rule of English. In fact, I contend that *not* splitting an infinitive often violates a crucial rule of English, and of any language: make your meaning clear.

The nuance if not the entire meaning of a sentence often depends on word placement, and if a word needs to squeeze between the "inseparable" components of an infinitive for clarity or other elements of communication, so be it. For instance, sometimes sentence flow is a strong reason to artfully split an infinitive. Place the words where they make the most sense, where they make the sentence smooth and clear.

Take, for example, these words from the penultimate sentence of the above paragraph: "to artfully split an infinitive." Where else might we place the word *artfully* so as to not split "to split" (and, rats, there I go splitting "to split" again).

• Flow is a strong reason to split an infinitive artfully.
• Flow is a strong reason to split artfully an infinitive.
• Flow is a strong and artful reason to split an infinitive.

The first version separates *artfully* from the word it is modifying, and weakens the sentence.

The second version rolls off the tongue the way a snoring drunk rolls off a barstool.

The third version converts *artfully* into an adjective and sends it off modifying something other than the craft of splitting.

---

[47] You don't speak Latin.
[48] You still don't speak Latin.

To split or not to split, *that* is the question. Writing that is true to itself and not to specious rules of grammar is the answer.

SPLIT INFINITIVES, PART 3

File under "To Gleefully Mock a Killing Bird": Making fun of the "Never split an infinitive" rule in three separate entries is not above me.

There's a reason that an obsolete meaning of *infinitive* is "an infinite amount," as the whole of our discussion of the split infinitive is now about to border on the infinitive.

Let's get down and dirty on the subject of split infinitives. The argument is that in Latin, infinitives were expressed in single words. And splitting a single word would be akin to splitting an absolute. *Tut-tut,* no splitting of absolutes. Well, watch me: *Abso-frikken-lute.* You can split *abso-frikken-lute* (*frikken* being an infix, in the spirit of suffix and prefix), so why can't you split two *separate* English words? You can toss words around in a sentence like a salad ("I am Sam, Sam I am, I do not like green eggs and ham"), so why do *to* and *go* in the infinitive *to go* have to cling together in perfect order like atoms in a molecule? Splitting infinitives is not nuclear fission, though doing so seems to set off thermonuclear devices in the rhetoric of some persnickitors.

When you declare that I'm worrying about this too much, I agree absolutely *and* abso-frikken-lutely, because we *all* are worrying about it too much. I speak in the entry above about how adherence to the rule can upset the rhythm of a sentence; perhaps more important is that it can upset the rhythm of the writer: "Oh, did I split that infinitive? And by the way, what the hell is an infinitive in the first place?"

So, if you're worrying more about keeping infinitives together as if you're a verbal marriage counselor and not a writer, a communicator, a normal speaker of English, you endanger comfortable rhythms of the communication itself. Yes, particularly in formal communication, we must understand and adhere to an array of rules and conventions with each keystroke, with each verbalization. But there's paying attention, and then there's being neurotic. Here I defer to the respected Mr. Francis George Fowler, coauthor of *Fowler's*[49] *Modern English Usage:*

> The English speaking world may be divided into (1) those who neither know nor care what a split infinitive is; (2) those who do not know, but care very much; (3) those who know & condemn; (4) those who know & approve; and (5) those who know & distinguish. Those who neither know nor care are the vast majority, & are a happy folk, to be envied by most of the minority classes.

And to definitively add quotational exclamation points, let me also bring in Mr. Raymond Chandler: "If I want to split an infinitive I'll damn well split an infinitive." And Mr. Norman Mailer: "If I split an infinitive, I mean to goddamn well split it." and Mr. *Oxford English Dictionary,* which cites this 1897 quote: "Are our critics aware that Byron is the father of their split infinitive? 'To slowly trace,' says the noble poet, 'the forest's shady scene.'"

ET CETERA
Not all English rules must be broken—unless, of course, they must, etc.

---

[49] Two Fowlers wrote the book, F.G. and brother Henry W. Should not the book's title technically be *Fowlers' Modern English Usage?*

Here's an English rule I encountered recently that I like: "When using Latin abbreviations in English, don't." Simple as that.

When deploying the *ibid.*s and the *viz.*s and the *vs.*s and the dozens of other Latin phrases we're subjected to in truncated and period-ended explication, you build yourself traps that you're certain to fall into yourself at one point or another. *I.e.,* you might misuse *i.e.,* as I just did. *I.e.* means "that is to say," and introduces a specific rephrasing of the point before. I should have used *e.g.,* which stands for "by way of example" (though in the context of abuse of Latin abbreviations, I also suggest that *e.g.* is a nice abbreviation of *egregious*). If you mean to say "for example," say "for example" and stop fretting over whether *i.e.* or *e.g.* is the appropriate confusing abbreviation. And if you mean to say "that is to say" or "in other words," think about restructuring your initial prose so that you don't have to immediately rephrase it.

In technical truncation (footnotes for scholarly papers, for instance), the convention of *cf.*s and *ibid.*s and *n.b.*s (nota who?) is perfectly appropriate. But scholarly papers are not the subject of this book, in that they are rarely written in anything recognizable as English. Jump beyond the simple confusion between *i.e.* and *e.g.*, and consider that *ibid.* sounds like a frog noise, and that *cf.* recalls a trendy modern-day abbreviation of a couple of earthy English words, even though *cf.* simply means "compare" (*cf.* slang from the Vietnam War and from the world of computer IT and from the Jon Stewart/*Daily Show* 2007-2008 series, *Clusterf@#k to the White House*).

One particular dangerous-territory Latin abbreviation is *et al.,* risky from a couple of standpoints. One is that it is regularly misabbreviated as I've just done it. *Et* is a complete word, but by analogy with the abbreviation that immediately follows it, it is often branded with a period. *Al.* is indeed an abbreviation, as in this example (e.g., i.e., r.s.v.p.): The book was written by George Burns, et al.

The translation, of course, is that the book was written by George Burns, *et* (meaning "and") *al.* (short for "Allen"). So *et al.* is a Burns and Allen routine (say *ibid.*, Gracie).

With all shtick aside, *al.* is an abbreviation of *alia*, and *et al.* means "and others" (*i.e.*, and oth.). But who knows that to the point of being able to navigate the figurative waters between Scylla and Charybdis (who are, yes I know, Greek).

Now, because this book is called *Everything You Know About English Is Wrong*, I must now contradict the very rule that I praised at the beginning of this entry: "When using Latin abbreviations in English, don't." Sometimes, do.

My two favorite uses of a Latin abbreviation appear in some quite popular media. Picture first bald and regal Yul Brynner declaring "Et setterah, et setterah, et setterah" in the musical *The King and I*. The pomposity of the King's use of *etc.* drives home another reason to eschew using Latin abbreviations in general text and conversation: it's pompous.

Next, bring to mind "Elenore," the '60s oldies hit from The Turtles (hint—rhyme "El" with "swell"). The entire song (in particular the lyric line "You're my pride and joy, et cetera") was intended to be a sarcastic dig at schmaltzy pop lyrics, as well as at the record company that demanded same from The Turtles. Such wonderful sarcasm I can appreciate, in the spirit of my condemning Latin abbreviations by earlier writing "as in the following example (e.g., i.e., r.s.v.p.)." The Turtles did it better.

Now, back to the original rule about using such dead-language abbreviations in our very vibrant language—just where did I find this advice? Check out the footnote.[50]

---

[50] *Cf. p. 34, ibid., v.* The Decline and Fall of the Roman Empire, *op. cit., c.v., c* spot run, run spot run, *r.b.i., c.d.* available on videocassette.

ET CETERA, ETC.
File under "Setterah, Et": Yul Brynner couldn't speak Latin. Or Thai, for that matter.

I spend an inordinate amount of time berating Latin abbreviations in English (weep for me, as it's a tough linguistic life) starting on page 149, though I admit that I backed off from my tirade in two cases involving Yul Brynner and The Turtles. I mention that here only to force people who have purchased this book to jump to the pages in question, or more important, to force people who have not purchased it to stop standing in the aisle blocking those who might be attracted to it, and head over to the checkout to plunk down some cash. Thank you. As I said, it's a tough linguistic life.

But back on point: In that specific elsewhere of this book, Yul inspired me to back off my tirade against Latin abbreviations because of his portrayal of the King of Siam in the Rodgers and Hammerstein musical *The King and I*.[51] At points in the play, the King intoned, "Et setterah, et setterah, et setterah," etc.

Now, if you're going to say *etc.* aloud without benefit of debonair baldness, Broadway costumes, or a snappy original-cast soundtrack album in the offing, pronounce it correctly. Saying "Et-sra" will do fine. Saying "And so on," will do finer, as it's English, while retaining the rhythm and implication you seek. Not the implication that Rodgers and Hammerstein sought, but for that we will forgive them. As with everything writing, use the tools at hand to best effect. Et setterah, et setterah, et setterah.

ΚριΤηιΛ—IS OR ARE?
Kappa Rho Iota Tau Eta Rho Iota Alpha is no longer an exclusive Greek Fraternity.

[51] Not *The King and Me*. There's no evidence that the first-person pronoun in the title is an object (in which case it is bad English grammar), or a subject (in which case it is good English grammar), but it's probably bad Siamese grammar either way.

The κριτηισυ I use for whether or not κριτηιλ is singular or plural is what language I happen to be speaking at the moment. If I'm speaking Ελληνικό then κριτηισυ is always the singular and κριτηιλ is always the plural. If, on the other hand, I'm speaking English, I will allow that *criteria* is acceptable as both singular and plural.

If all that is Ελληνικό to you, I empathize, as it's all *Hellenic*— Greek—to me, too, especially the part about forcing the word *criteria* to be plural only. But I composed that paragraph just as was done in the 1600s when we brought κριτηιλ into English: I used Greek letters to write the words *criterion* and *criteria*. The writers at the time acknowledged that the borrowed word was indeed foreign and played according to foreign rules. As the word became more common, it conformed to the English convention of using the Roman alphabet. Simply put, the word became English. Why, then, can't the words also be allowed to conform to other English conventions?

English allows words to be both singular and plural—*deer, minutia,*[52] *moose, news*—*criteria* can settle in line, as well.

And if that bothers some folks, I care not one ioton and certainly not two iotas.

KUDOS

Giving someone a kudo is not bad English—bad Greek, maybe, but not bad English.

If I were to—for whatever bizarre reason—want to praise a pea, I could give a kudo to a pea.

---

[52] Interestingly, the first recorded use of *minutia* in English (in 1782) refers to "some little minutias"—prophetic considering I didn't write this book of minutias until nearly a quarter millennium later.

The screaming would come immediately: "Illiterate!," the persnickitors will shout at me. "*Kudos* might mean 'congratulations,' but it is a singular word. You don't create the singular by removing the S from *kudos!*"

All right, then. If I am to play by that particular rule, I will apply Xtreme Etymological Stasis and praise a pea by giving kudos to a pease. The screaming would be different this time: "What the hell is a pease?"

So let me counter the screaming: If converting *kudos* to the singular by dropping the S is such a linguistic sin, why have we allowed it with *pease* (in various forms back to about A.D. 800), the original singular form of *pea*, an S-less word that didn't show up until around the early 1600s? (*Pease* was also a plural form, just as *moose* is both singular and plural.)

So here's the scorecard, according to some:

Kudo instead of *kudos*: substandard English (and spoken substandardly since by the mid-1920s).

Pea instead of *pease*: standard English.

Cherry instead of *cherise*: standard English. (At least with *cherry* we created it wrong in the first place. *Cherise* is Old Northern French borrowed into English by 1300. Again, we thought that dropping an S would give us a singular. Good thing we didn't apply that reasoning to a couple of the words used above: *moo* wouldn't make a particularly good singular for *moose*, and *rai* wouldn't be an efficient synonym for one instance of *raise*.)

So, kudos to the careful writers who still use *pease*, and a *kudo* to those who eat all their peas and believe that this language is flexible enough, permissive enough, to allow us to use *kudo*.

A side note: the creation of *kudo* on the model of *pea* demonstrates—ironically—that everything old is news again, given the fact that a *new* was a singular instance of something new, but now we use that noun only in its plural—*news*—which we regard as singular. And for that we can give a prai.

DEBT

File under "B, Spelling": *Debt* is undoubtedly subtly misspelled.

I've participated in my share of spelling bees over the years, getting my backside kicked off the stage for such transgressions as inserting an *E* into the final syllable of *Septuagint.* I should have just stood there and said, "Septuagint. G-I-M-N-illiterate. Septuagint." I've obviously never won a spelling bee.

Spelling bees are pretty much an English-speaking event, because other languages are much more consistent with spelling convention. Holding a spelling bee for a language with strong adherence to phonetics would be something akin to having a math bee in which contestants rattle off the numerals for a given number. "Bill, your number is one thousand and one."

I clear my throat, ask for and receive a definition of one thousand and one, ask for and receive an alternate pronunciation, then inquire about the origin ("Arabic numerals, stupid!" someone shouts from the audience). Then I say, "One thousand and one. One-Zero-Zero-One. One thousand and one." And then, because I left out the comma after the first *one,* I am booted off the stage, left to ponder what the heck a Septuagint is.

All that is long lead-in to a letter that centuries ago was injected artificially into English words, and therefore into spelling bees. That letter is, of course, *B*.

Let's take the word *debt*. We pronounce it "det." At one time, as late as the mid 1500s, we even spelled it *det*. Or variations thereof, like *dett* and *dette*. So where did *B* come marching into the bee? When "learned" monks transliterating manuscripts decided that the Latin origins of that word (related to *debit*) demanded a *B* to make it "truer" to its origins, as well as to, yes, make it simpler. "There was a genuine belief that it would help people if they could 'see' the original Latin in a Latin-derived English word," writes David Crystal in *The Fight for English* (who then points out the people being helped were originally spelled peple, before an O was injected in a similar attempt to reflect Latin populous). We also owe our spelling of *subtle, doubt,* and (of all things) *plumber* to such actions. Me, I think the monks changed the spellings so that bad spellers could last longer in spelling bees to drive audience interest, the way they keep bad singers around for so many episodes of *American Idol*.

OK, enough ranting about this subject. I'm just going to lebt it B.[53]

---

[53] An aside that has nothing to do with anything. I'd love to see a spelling bee in which one of the words is "BB, a small pellet projectile used in air rifles," just so we could hear the featured speller announce: "BB. B-B. BB."

Oh, Stop Being So Cranky, or I'll Give You Something to Be Cranky About

I suppose it's a common Mom-ism—at the very least, my mother Momized me with it enough times over the years: "Stop your crying or I'll give you something to cry about."

Herein, I'm going to Momize a few persnickitors. When they whine about the use of certain words, you can give them something further to whine about. It's somewhat of a game of "Well, if you're going to play by those rules, let's follow them to their logical conclusion." In other words, we are here going to fully exercise to the fun game of Xtreme Etymological Stasis (which, to reiterate, is abbreviated XeS and pronounced "excess").

COHORT

File under "Hort, Co-": A cohort is not a single person—yet.

Cohort is a singular noun encompassing a plurality, much like such words as *entourage, team, cortege, retinue,* and *posse.* Your cohort is the group around you. Yet, the word is frequently misused to refer to a single person: "I'm Bill, and this is my cohort, George."

Such use is akin to me saying, "I'm Bill, and this is my entourage, George." That may not be as ridiculous as it sounds, because you can, I suppose, have an entourage of one (though I personally can't drum up an entourage that numbers even that many) and therefore, by technical extension a possible cohort of one. However, *cohort* becomes ungrammatical when people start saying "these are my cohorts, George and Libby." (Compare "these are my entourages, George and Libby.")

But the people who commit such misuses and their cohorts are eventually going to win. Yes. Their *cohorts* are going to win. Live with it.

They're going to win because language changes. If you want to demand that the word cohort remain static, then revert to Xtreme Etymological Stasis and use the word in its original meaning. If I were doing just that, I would be saying, "I'm Bill, and this is my cohort, Julius, Claudius, Spartacus, Brutus, Snuffleupagus, and 295 other Roman legionnaires." *Cohort* is a historical military term describing a tenth of a legion, at least 300 soldiers (that's CCC soldiers, give or take I or II, if you want to truly adhere to Xtreme Etymological Stasis). Recently, this ancient military term has been used figuratively to describe colleagues and companions in general.

Colleague and *companion*—lurking within those synonyms lies the other reason that the cohorts will win. As we've seen frequently on these pages, English follows patterns . . . well, relatively often . . . OK, occasionally. English speakers often "misinterpret" words by viewing them according to patterns and precedents and similarities. In this case, the first syllable of *cohort* has mild but distinct resonances with words like *colleague* and *companion* (fueled by the similarity in meaning), and *hard* resonances with words like *co-author, co-captain,* and the established and self-redundant *co-conspirator.*

With that in mind, I predict that we will eventually see one or both of two possible further corruptions of *cohort.* Like *co-conspirator,* we could see in generations to come the word *co-cohort.* More likely, we'll see a dissection of cohort:

"I'm Bill, and this is my *hort,* George. In fact, George and I are co-horts."

DECIMATE, PART I

"In this world, nothing can be said to be certain, except decimation."—*almost said by Benjamin Franklin, 1789*

We've heard the ponderous announcements from our always
deeply concerned TV news crews dozens of times. Variations of
"The tornado swept through without warning, decimating the
small town!"

Persnickitors take umbrage when hearing such use. "The
word *decimate*," they declare, "is not synonymous with the word
destroy!" And indeed it isn't. "*Decimate*," they declare, "refers to
the Roman army's practice of punishing mutineers or deserters
by decimating . . . um . . . killing or severely beating one tenth of
the group, chosen by lot." And indeed, that is one meaning. Still,
the righteous persnickitors might not have any foundation for
feeling superior to our deeply concerned TV news crews when it
comes to precision. You see, decimation is the taking of a
tenth—*deca* being Latin for "ten." The word *decimation* was
applied to the rare Roman practice, but it was hardly the sole
meaning of the word in Latin.

Nor, for that matter, in English. Neither the sole meaning nor
even the *original* meaning. And here's where we reintroduce Mr.
Franklin and our mangling of his quote that introduced this entry.
Yes, *decimation* in English describes the Roman military punish-
ment, but such description is not the first English use of the word.
Decimation first came to English by the middle of the sixteenth
century meaning "tithing or taxation at the rate of one tenth."

So meanings of *decimation* of which we can be certain, are . . .
death . . . *and* taxes.[54]

---

[54] Briefly returning to the travails of our small town, using *decimate* might actually be true to
the meaning of punishing every tenth one, given the capricious nature of tornados—picking
up random cars out of an otherwise undamaged parking lot and flinging them half way
across the county. But the possibility of such precise use is likely being overly gracious to our
deeply concerned TV news crews.

DECIMATE, PART II
Your intrepid author can't leave this topic alone.

After confirming that *decimate* and *destroy* are not synonyms (see "Decimate, Part I," above) because *decimate* means the taking of a tenth, I must backtrack to point out a rare but recorded nineteenth-century use of *decimation*: Edward A. Freeman writes in *Historical and Architectural Sketches; Chiefly Italian*, "A systematic decimation of the surviving male adults. By decimation is here meant the slaying, not of one out of ten, but of nine out of ten."

THE SAHARA DESERT, PART II
The quibbling continues.

If I write, "The Sahara Desert is in north Africa," persnickitors will bellow, "That's redundant! To be technical, *Sahara* means 'desert' in Arabic, so you're really saying 'The Desert Desert.' Say 'The Sahara is in north Africa.'" As I point out on page 31, this doesn't bother me. But if it bothers you, then, once again, we must apply some Xtreme Etymological Stasis in the spirit of my grousing about *hoi polloi* on page 29. To be even more technical, the name of that vast stretch of no apple trees, mulberry bushes, or McDonald's is *as-sahra,* "The Great Desert." If you insist that I say "The Sahara is in north Africa," then I invoke XeS and insist that *you* say simply "Sahara is in north Africa," to avoid using words that ultimately translate to "The the Great Desert."

Satisfied?

LIGHT/LITE, NIGHT/NITE

File under "Lite Bombastic, Tripping the": *Lite* is not an abomination.

In 1975, the Miller Brewing Company was engaged in a battle that
attracted almost as much attention as its *less-filling!-tastes-great!*
arguments waged in the legendary Miller Lite beer commercials
(and likely involving even more shouting). Miller contended that
other beers marketed as "Brand X Light" were violating Miller's
trademarked *Lite*, with its unique spelling, and instigated lawsuits
against seven competitors.

Meantime, other rumblings were, um, brewing. Lite's growing
popularity provoked outrage not from the T-totalers but from the
L-I-G-H-T-totalers. Fuming at this abominable intentional
misspelling, the L-I-G-H-T-totalers seemed certain that our nation's
youth would be leaving the streets strewn not with empty beer cans
but with ignored silent *G-H* letter combinations. Of course, such
alarm over modernized and seemingly illiterate respellings has
been around for years, and a related target has been "misspelling"
night as *nite*.

Of course, Miller was wrong. About the lawsuit, anyway. In
1977, a U.S. circuit court ruled: "because 'light' is a generic or
common descriptive word when applied to beer, neither that word
nor its phonetic equivalent may be appropriated as a trademark for
beer." And Miller was oddly right. About the spelling, that is. *Light*
and *night* are of course very old words, tracing back to Old English.
Yet, the silent *G* in each word is not native to its spelling; it was
added around the 1300s. Early spellings of the adjective *light*, the
opposite of *heavy*, include (in alphabetical and not chronological
order) *léoht, leht, leicht, leyt, lighte, lihht, liht, lihte, lit, lite, lixt, lycht,*

lyht, lyt, lyte, lyth. The orthographical cornucopia of *night* spelling variants is far more extensive. So, yes, *lite* is not a currently accepted spelling, but then again it is perhaps closer to the word's original spelling than our currently accepted variant.

By the way, Miller Lite commercials claimed that the brew had "a third less calories," which of course had the L-I-G-H-T-totalers responding, "You mean 'a third *fewer*' calories," as calories are countable items and not amorphous amounts. In the land of word history, however, that would have smacked of redundancy. Though unrelated to *light,* the now obsolete word *lite,* tracing back to Old English, meant "few." Maybe that's the *Lite* that Miller Brewing had in mind all along.

FIGURATIVE/LITERAL

File under "Figure 8 (ively)": "Literally speaking" is not a figure of speech.

If I were to say in exasperation, "I was literally climbing the walls," the persnickitors might very well respond, "I was *figuratively* climbing the walls!" both to correct me and to express their own exasperation with dorks who confuse the concepts of "literally" and "figuratively." People regularly (and the persnickitors say incorrectly) use the word *literally* to express figuratism. If you figuratively climb the walls, you are agitated/frustrated/crazy. If you literally climb the walls, you are Spiderman.

But even literally climbing the walls can be figurative. Here's my logic. If I say, "I was climbing the walls," you understand that I mean it in the figurative sense. You don't picture me with suction cups on my hands and feet, delusionally declaring myself to be Peter Parker while climbing the second of two stories of the J.D.

Johnssen Business Miniplex and All-Night Dry Cleaners in Powhattan, Kansas (besides, no one proved that about me in court). My statement declares the literal. You infer and therefore understand the figurative. This is what we call hyperbole.

Now, if I say, "I was literally climbing the walls," I am still declaring (though more specifically) the literal. But suddenly you stop inferring and understanding the figurative, misled by the semantic use of the word *literal* and not considering its possible communicative use. Perhaps I meant to intensify my exasperation with an adverb intensifying the climb. How, I ask, is "I was really really really climbing the walls" any different than "I was literally climbing the walls"?

Besides, how could anyone possibly interpret my saying "I was literally climbing the walls" as a confession that I was once again bringing out the suction cups (and consequently further payments to my lawyer)? Persnickitors understand what I mean (it is still, after all, hyperbole), yet they choose to concentrate on *how* I expressed the thought while ignoring *what* I expressed. This is somewhat akin to telling Dick Fosbury, who introduced the then-bizarre backward high jump to track and field, "Yeah, you leaped over that high-jump bar, but it doesn't count 'cuz you flopped."

Granted, I'm being argumentative. I myself am always careful to distinguish between the words *figuratively* and *literally* in writing and speaking. Yet, there are other things to consider about this "mistake."

Consideration #1: The precedented flip-flopping of words expressing the figurative vs. the literal. A virtual cornucopia of words originally expressing reality now express figuratism. And you see the hyperbole in that previous sentence, don't you? The phrase "virtual cornucopia" connotes exaggeration, yes? Especially since a cornucopia is a mythical object. But . . .

The original "literal" meaning of *virtual* connoted physical presence or influence, kind of a cousin of the word *visceral*. That meaning goes back to the late 1300s, when our modern holographic-tinted phrase "virtual reality" might actually be understood, though would probably be considered redundant.

The meaning of *virtual* has kind of flip-flopped—literally *and* figuratively. In that context, also consider "veritable cornucopia."

Consideration #2: The literal interpretation of the word *literal*. If we're to be so persnickitorially literal in our use of *literal,* then let's employ the rule of Xtreme Etymological Stasis, beyond and backward of what the speaker intends the word to mean, and back to what the word originally, actually, virtually, veritably meant in the first place. If you were literally "literally" climbing "the walls," you would be clambering over ascenders and serifs and other thorny obstacled rungs on the ladder formed by the letters *T, H, E, W, A, 2 L's,* and an *S.* You see, to be *literal,* in the literal sense, is to be involved with letters. The ABC type letters.

Now, another literal expression might be (suction cups not needed) "I was walking the walls—literally." An early obsolete meaning of *literally* was "alliterative." Woo-woo! We walk the walls! Literally, of course.

DATA
File under "Data and other minutia": If you can't beat 'em, datum.

As you've surmised from some of the entries in this book, I'm a baseball fan. Like so many fans, I participate in fantasy baseball leagues, where minutia rules. One of my leagues in particular is unusual in that it uses many arcane statistics beyond roster maximums, batting averages, runs scored, and the like. The league also considers the effects of stadiums on players—grass vs. artificial turf, amount of foul territory, distance to the outfield walls, etc. Now, this arcane data is . . .

"Stop, Mr. Brohaugh!," I hear the persnickitors shout (though the real shouts aren't quite that polite). "First of all, you're boring us to tears! But more important, the word *data* is plural! You should say that the arcane data 'are,' not 'is'!"

OK, time to take a breath. Let's for the moment forget that no one discussing baseball, with beer in hand and ESPN blaring in the background, is going to utter "the data are" in public without attracting deserved ridicule. Instead, let's concentrate on the likelihood that many if not most of the persnickitors did *not* start their shouting when I used the plural *minutia* with a singular verb form, and used the plural forms *minimums* and *stadiums* instead of *minima* and *stadia*.

Let's either demand absolute consistency in the spirit of Xtreme Etymological Statis, or allow that our vastly irregular language can survive additional irregularities.

The technical singular of *data* is *datum*. There it is, one datum, as tiny and identifiable as one bacterium. "Look at this fascinating datum I discovered, Mr. Poindexter." Now that sounds like a sentence you hear every day, doesn't it? Add another datum, and you have two data. One po-datum, two po-data, three po-data, four.

And why don't those who insist that we use *data* as the plural of *datum* also insist that we use *minima* and *stadia* as the plurals of *minimum* and *stadium*?

Now, likely some of you are ready to jump down my throat for some etymological errors in the above discussion, errors that I threw out as red herrings. *Minutia* properly carries a singular verb form, because the word is both singular and plural. Interestingly, however, the word was pluralized as *minutias* for a time when it was brought into English in the 1700s. And in the context of allowing one minutia to become two minutias in English (the way we speak of two or more militias), I contend that refusing to recognize *data* as a singular because it violates Latin grammar amounts to refusing it full citizenship in the English language, where it can perform as it wants to without having to pay taxes to the Old Country.

Knowledge comprises many facts. Data comprises many details. We have developed a sense of *data* as encompassing a body of information. This particular use of *data* is, in essence, *a new word,* and therefore, free from the history of its immigrant parents *datum* and *data.* I return to my fantasy baseball league, and an example I use elsewhere in this book: When a batter hits a pop fly to left field, we say he *flies out* present tense, *flied out* past tense. In this sense, *fly* is a different word than the one whose past tense is expressed with *flew.*

So, this *data-is-plural* trivia deserves to be ignored. Yes, *deserves* singular even though *trivia* is technically plural.

And speaking of trivia, let me tell you about the .425 on-base percentage my fantasy league batters had through May of last year, with a strikeout-to-walk ratio of [continued on page 876].

Y'ALL
Y'all is not bad English, y'all.

I'm a Yankee by birth, but I've spent enough time with Southern friends to have picked up occasional use of *y'all.* I'm certain my

twang-inflection of the word amuses or irritates those friends no
end. I might have chosen *you'ns,* which is more colloquially
Northern, or *youse,* or the phrase that seems to more commonly
express the same sentiment: "You guys."[55]

Yes, all these forms are informal, but just like *ain't,* they exhibit
good English grammar in that they are *necessary* English forms,
filling holes left by shifting meanings and word uses.

Y'all and its kin indicate second person plural—more than one you.
Once upon a time, the phrase "more than one you" would have been
redundant, as *you* and companion word *ye* were used exclusively to
indicate second person plural. The old word for the second person
singular was *thou* (and *thee* as an object). It's easier to see this in
an example:

• Thou give to me. I give to thee.
• Ye give to us. We give to you.

But *thou/thee* began to communicate familiarity (much like *du*
vs. *Sie* in German), and eventually to communicate disdain, so thou
and I stopped using those words and turned to the plural pronouns
ye/you to replace *thou/thee.* And eventually *you*—you usurper,
you—replaced *ye,* as well (now performing the work of four
pronouns with no likely raise in salary—talk about downsizing).
But that leaves some unclarity, with no specific word indicating the
second person plural exclusively. A void, which *y'all* have stepped in
to fill. And for that, I thank *you* and *ye* and *thee* and *thou*—for not
having to return *thee* and *thou* to the lexicon, I thank *y'all.*

---

[55] Often expanded to "Youse guys," perhaps applied to larger groups.

English Is Not from England, and Other Little Surprises

We speak many verbs that originated from French. In a way, *all* verbs are French, in that the word *verb* itself came to us from that language—as did many of the words describing English sentences. From French itself also came *adjective, adverb,* and (*sacre bleu!*) *interjection!*—and from Anglo-Norman and Middle French came such words as *noun, pronoun,* and (not to keep you dangling) *participle.*

Prefix? Latin. And *suffix,* too.

And creating the word *gerund* was borrowing Latin, as well.

The word *English?* Oh, it's English. Old English, in fact. But not British. For more on that, and some peeks into the components of our non-British language that may contradict your assumptions, let's speak . . .

ENGLISH (THE LANGUAGE)

File under "Biting the Mother Tongue": *English* does not come from England.

The mother tongue does not come from Mother England. Rather, it invaded from across the North Sea, when around 450 A.D. West Germanic tribes filled the invasion void left when the Romans abandoned Britain for more easily defensible lands some forty years previous. Among these tribes were the Angles and the Saxons, who spoke languages likely quite similar, languages that eventually became known in aggregate as *Englisc*—Angle-ish—

what we now refer to as Old English or Anglo-Saxon. Old English is in many ways really old Germanic.

England—the name now synonymous with *Britain*—comes from the *Angle land,* or at least the new, conquered Land of the Angles (and the Saxons, the Jutes, and the rest, here on Angle-Land's Isle). So, *English* does not come from England. *England* comes from the English.

ADJECTIVE
An adjective was first an adjective, not a noun.

An adjective is something of a turncoat. When borrowed from French around the early 1400s, *adjective* was the adjective in the phrase "noun adjective" (for a clearer grasp on this, stress the second syllable, as you would the word *objective*). It was apparently so impressed with its companion noun *noun* that it came to the dark side, Luke, and now works almost exclusively as a noun.

NONCE-WORD
Nonce-word is not.

A nonce-word is one created "for the nonce," for a specific one-time occasion or use. For instance, if I were to declare much of the word-play in this book as my personal for-the-moment *noncence,* I'd be creating a nonce-word, a pun on *nonsense.* It's said that longtime *Oxford English Dictionary* editor James Murray created it in 1884 (well, the *Oxford English Dictionary* is among those that said it, so it's probably true).

My favorite nonce-word comes from Joseph Kell's novel *Inside Mr Enderby*: "The intermittent drone was finneganswaked by lightly sleeping Enderby into a parachronic lullaby chronicle." Kell is what we might call a *nonce-de-plume,* a pen name used once by one Anthony Burgess, author of *A Clockwork Orange*, the novel filled with a concocted dialect called *nadsat*. Burgess as Kell using the name of James Joyce's nonce-terpiece *Finnegans Wake* to create a nonce-verb . . . ah, the artifice is simply delicious. (The Joseph Kell pseudonym was apparently so well hidden that the *Yorkshire Post* sent a copy of *Inside Mr Enderby* to Burgess to review; Burgess shrugged, did not say "What the Kell?" and proceeded to review his own book.)

Meanwhile, back to the topic at hand: the word *nonce-word,* once itself a nonce-word, is no longer itself, as we now use it all the time.

And that nonessential fact is also a noncential fact.[56]

CAN

File under "Can can't always": *Can* is not a complete verb.

Certain verbs are like my computer printer after I fixed it. It's as if they were taken apart, cleaned up a little, put back together, and then operate nicely while the amateur printer-fixer wonders what those little spokey parts are that never found their way back into the machinery. And then, like the printer I had to replace, the words stop. Because these certain verbs are missing some parts. They are defective.

Can is a defective verb. So are *ought, must, may, will, shall,* and others. But, you say, you use them every day. How can they work if they're broken, if they're defective?

---

[56] Another noncential fact is that the word *nonce* is not derived from the word *once*. *Once* is a mistaken reformation of words in the Middle English phrase "for then anes," meaning "for a single purpose."

Consider the following quick demonstration, using the word *demonstrate* itself. We begin simply: "I demonstrate." Two further conjugations are

1. He demonstrates.
2. He is demonstrating.

Now, perform the same conjugation with this sentence: "I should demonstrate."

1. He should demonstrate.
2.

Yes, nothing follows "2." because there is no "He is shoulding demonstrate." *Should* is a defective verb. It's not really broken— "defective" is technical linguistic terminology to define words that don't have all the possible forms as the other words, and thus are in therapy to try to recover their self-esteem.[57]

HYPHENS, AS OPPOSED TO DASHES
Shorter is not shorter, and longer is not longer.

One day while listening to the radio, I was oddly jolted when the drive-time talk-show host announced the website address of that day's guest. "That's Unfortunate English dot com . . . specifically, Unfortunate hyphen English dot com."

I looked at the radio, and nearly whispered, "He got it right."

The little vertically suspended punctuation mark (-) between connected words is indeed a *hyphen*. And this sentence ends with a hyphenated-word. This is opposed to a *dash,* the wider-shouldered vertically suspended punctuation mark (—) that connects not words, but phrases and clauses. English speakers seem to be losing their grasp of the distinction.

---

[57] Then there's the computer printer that I broke by adding in too many parts (well, I never did such a thing, but let's not mix analogies). Consider the ugly new verb we're seeing on computer screens: *login,* as in "Click here and login." The preposition has been added to *log,* creating the now defective verb *login.* I login, you login, he . . . he . . . damn! He broke that one, too. (For more on this particular rant, see "Hell oh Hell," on page 211.)

Fittingly, the example that jolted me is also an example of why people forget about or perhaps even ignore the once-venerable hyphen. The talk-show host was delineating an address for the Internet, where the revered period has been descriptively relabeled a "dot." That, frankly, doesn't bother me, as *dot* not only is easier to say in a time when we're swapping web and email addresses nearly hourly, but also clearly communicates the function of our cute little punctuational speck. After all, we don't refer to the dot in dollar figures as a period. It is clearly tagged a *decimal point.*

But in those cases, a dot is a dot is a dot. A hyphen is not a dash, nor a dash a hyphen. But the same verbal shorthand that reduced *period* to *dot* generally has people inflating the shorter-thing-longer-word *hyphen* into the longer-thing-shorter-word *dash.* Had Mr. Talk Show said "Unfortunate dash English dot com," I likely would have simply shrugged mentally and thought, as I've done occasionally, "Heaven forfend you ever encounter an underscore, and thank God we've stopped using tildes in web addresses." Once again, with people engaged so heavily in web-speak (and not web—speak) and email address exchanges, I'm fully expecting the everyday English speaker's distinction between *dash* and *hyphen* to fade, while I take solace that people haven't taken to referring to the major punctuation symbols as *comma, colon,* and *dot.* Not yet, at least.

As an aside, the word *hyphen* comes from Greek, ultimately from a word meaning "together." The Greek hyphen itself was a kind of U symbol placed *underneath* the connected words, which I consider to be punctuational poetry. But it would make for some pretty confusing website addresses . . .

OXYMORON

File under "Moron, Oxy": Not all oxymorons are
nonsensical.

An oxymoron is a figure of speech or a style of argumentation that
combines seemingly disparate elements, and we often think of it as
a self-contradicting phrase. George Carlin used "jumbo shrimp" as
an example (one that the literate Mr. Carlin may not realize is even
more oxymoronic when you consider that the word *shrimp* is
related to words meaning "shrivel," including *scrimp*, difficult to do
when buying high-priced jumbo shrimp).

But the idea of an apparent oxymoron that makes sense? You
might think that that bizarre notion comes out of left field. Nope.
In fact, the original Greek word denotes intentionally making a
point by utilizing incongruity, something of the type of opposite
approach employed in sarcasm or facetiousness.

That's on a higher philosophical level. On a more granular
word-by-word level, you'll regularly find instances of apparently
contradictory words working harmoniously. For instance, that
bizarre notion of coming out of left field. It didn't come out of left
field because it's still "out in" left field.

PNEUMONOULTRAMICROSCOPICSILICO-
VOLCANOCONIOSIS

File under "-*osis, Pneumonoultramicroscopicsilicovolcanoconi*":
"*Pneumonoultramicroscopicsilicovolcanoconiosis* is not the
longest word in the English language, but is the longest word
my poor typesetters have to deal with at this moment.

OK, *Pneum-etc.* is a word. And, yup, it's a long one. But it's a word that was made up purely to be a long word. The *Oxford English Dictionary* says that it's likely the creation of one Everett M. Smith, who served as president of the National Puzzlers' League in 1935. It even has a "meaning": black-lung disease, for us laypeople.

Yes, every word is a made-up word, but if we were to accept this as a real word and then crown it the longest word in the language, we might as well allow me to type at random for several hundred pages without spaces and declare two things: (1) that what I'd just typed is now the world's longest word, and (2) that suddenly I've met my page-count commitment for the length of this book, saving me a whole lot of work.

Still, even if we concede that *pneumonoultra-and-ensuing-train-wreck* is a real word, it would not the longest word in English.

You can find examples of some plenty long words that have appeared in texts, including *honorificabilitudinitatibus*, from the same writer who gave us such shorter treasures as *majestic, multi-tudinous,* and (ironically) *frugal*: William Shakespeare. But *honor-yadayada* is not the longest word in the language. Nor are the sumptuously syllablized technical terms nor the longlonglong Welsh place names the longest.

You see, the longest word in the English language is *sesquipedalian,* even though it has but fourteen letters and six syllables.

It means "the use of big words," but it doesn't seem to be the biggest of the big—until you analyze its origin. Latin, of course: *sesqui-*, meaning one and a half, and *-pedalian,* "of the foot," from Horace's phrase *sesquipedalia verba. Sesquipedalian* is the longest word in the English language, measuring a full foot and a half.

With exquisite appropriateness, *sesquipedalian* grew a toe and a bunion from its earlier, shorter form: *sesquipedal.* But if the shoe doesn't fit . . .

ETYMOLOGY

For future reference, this one is good to know:

Etymology (the history of words) and *entomology* (the study of insects) are different. This brings to mind two conclusions.

1. I know, I know: you knew that.
2. The computer's search and replace function saved me an awful lot of time on the second draft of this book.

THESAURUS

You say there's no other word for *thesaurus?* I say, wrong, incorrect, awry, untrue, false, off-target, inexact, inaccurate, mistaken, counterfactual, specious, ungrounded, spurious, ixnay, not!

It's a classic one-liner associated with comedian Steven Wright, whose delivery makes monotone seem operatic: "What's another word for *thesaurus?*" Clever line. Bad etymology.

The word *thesaurus* has numerous synonyms—so many that you could fill a magazine with them. So many you could fill a warehouse with them. A storehouse even, or perhaps a treasury, a depository, a repository, an armory, a stockpile, a chest, a compendium, a vault, a hoard, a promptuary, a reservoir . . . all of which, you have likely guessed by now, are words that you would legitimately find in a thesaurus of thesauri.

Our word *thesaurus* came to us ultimately from Greek, through Latin and then through Roget. But let's back up a few centuries before Mr. Roget stepped in with his innovative and much-celebrated word organization. In Greek, the word was *thesauros*, meaning "treasury or the treasure within," "storehouse," and "chest." In Latin, the word was spelled as we spell it now, which you should regret because it opened me up to that sad *thesauri* joke above.

When the word came to English in the 1500s, it had primarily figurative use as a collection of knowledge—so, in that sense, *dictionary* is another word for *thesaurus*, and so is *encyclopedia*. Peter Mark Roget's particular collection of knowledge—grouping similar words by ideas—could well have been published as a *Treasury of English Words and Phrases*, but a synonym for *treasury* was chosen instead. Over the years, the book was so successful (Roget himself supervised more than a dozen subsequent editions over the next seventeen years until his death in 1869) that the meaning of *thesaurus* was narrowed to a specific type of collection.

Now, when I first said you could fill a magazine with *thesaurus* synonyms, I meant *magazine* as a synonym of *warehouse* or *storehouse*, which was the original meaning of the word—and a meaning that remains. A print magazine is a treasury or collection of articles, just as a gun magazine is a collection of bullets. Some years back, a media commentator, apparently forgetting that he owned a dictionary, fumed over CBS's *60 Minutes* calling itself a "television magazine." Magazine it is, as it collects things—stories. And you could even call *60 Minutes* a television thesaurus.

Now, I'm wondering (and I'm certain that I'm not the first): What if you don't know the meaning of *dictionary?* Or did Steven Wright already beat me to that line?[58]

---

[58] Hmm, because *thesaurus* is ultimately a Greek word, should we should respell it as *hoisaurus* . . . (see "Hoi Polloi" on page 29 for my smarmy explanation of that little jibe).

LINGUISTIC TERMINOLOGY
Technical language terms are not based on curse words.

Well, nobody but me has ever claimed that they are—I'm just being "accusative" here, which is leading to the theme of this little note: I think much of linguistic technical terminology would make some effective educated, noninsulting taunting. *Ow, you hit me, you diphthong! You spirant! I'm bringing out the plosives! Frick a tiv!* In fact, *fricative* may be disappearing from the high school English-class curriculums (if it hasn't already died out of pure disuse), given the seeming rise of the euphemism *frikken* to replace . . . well, not *fricative,* and given the likelihood that the very word inspires snickers and even snickratives . . .

COMMA FAULTS
The common comma, is prone t,o mis,,use

I begin nearly every speech at writers conferences by stressing that only One Rule applies in writing. This rule is true—and it's mandated—at every book publisher, every magazine office, every PR and ad agency. It's true in poetry, in fiction, in nonfiction, in instructional manuals. It's true in writing both formal and informal. And that rule is: *Never start a sentence with a comma.*

Even though I've anticipated it, I've received no argument about this advice lo the many years I've been using the tongue-in-cheek ice-breaker. Why have I anticipated argument? Because I've seen in print numerous instances where my edict has been broken with no apparent respect for The One Rule. (One of those instances was not a book called *Comma Eats Comma Shoots Comma and Leaves*

Comma Comma, though I'm thinking of using that as the title of my next project.)

I know that you, as well, have seen instances of The One Rule being broken. I know because you've read this far. Glance up to the first sentence of the second paragraph, directly above. You see

Even though I've anticipated it,

You've spotted the comma, correct?—the one that does not begin the sentence but in fact ends the phrase? Of course. It's obvious. But do you recognize the comma that *does* begin the sentence? In fact, the highlighted series of characters above embodies *two* commas. One is the punctuation mark that we call a comma. The other is the phrase "Even though I've anticipated it," which, curiously, is also a comma.

The first use of the word *comma* in English was a borrowing from Latin and Greek. A comma was a short phrase, not quite a sentence. (In fact, the *OED* gives as the definition of Greek comma "a piece cut off," which might make a good model for people looking to tighten their prose.) The word *comma* in this definition, tracing back to ancient literature and in use in English by the 1500s, was subsequently transferred to the punctuation symbol that set off the short phrase, the piece cut off.

As an aside, that particular symbol has not always been the little descendent apostrophe that you've already seen twenty-seven times in this entry, and now twenty-eight times, and now . . . OK, stop that. Various symbols have been used to offset commas-as-phrases, including what we now call the slash, forward-slash (computer times, and all), or the virgule (/), the use of which survives in today when quoting poetry within prose: "I think that I shall never see/ a poem lovely as a tree." But the virgule kind of slipped down on the page, squinched up, and started to dribble below the line. I blame global warming, which melted the virgule into the present symbol. If you can't stand the heat/ get out of the kitchen.

, that said/ I'm done with this entry/ except to say that you should never end a sentence with a comma/ either,[59]

---

[59] ,nor, for that matter, an entire book section,

Animal Farm

Dr. Dolittle meets George Orwell. Let us talk to the animals, though I wonder if Orwell can almost sing as well as Rex Harrison in the classic musical and non–Eddie Murphy version of the Dolittle tale.

Beware, though, as the animals talk back to us, we're going to lose our G rating in this section, with the expected barnyard humor:

ASININE

What's the answer to "Got a match?" Hint: "My ass and your donkey" is not a clever response.

One of the most asinine etymologies I've heard is that *ass*—as in *donkey*—is the source of the pejorative word *asinine* itself— meaning "obstinate, crass, silly."

Well, of course it's an asinine etymology, first because it's about the word *asinine* and second because it's right. But, you say, everybody knows that *asinine* refers to the human bottom, and being asinine is being a figurative asshole—a jerk, a dolt. Alas and an ass, what everybody knows is (shock upon shock) wrong. *Asinine* means "related to what we now refer to as a donkey," in the same formation as *feline, canine, porcine,* and *forktine,* though I'll admit that the last one was added just so I could be asinine. Again.

PUSSYFOOT

File under "Foot, P-Word": *Pussyfoot* is not a bad word.

I was in the audience at Memphis's FedEx Arena, watching, of all things, a prize fight (lightweight championship of the world, mind you). I was not there doing research for this book, but if I mention it here, perhaps I can use that trip to Memphis as a tax write-off. Somewhere around the ninth round, a woman behind me began getting restless. Neither fighter was taking control of the bout. The woman wanted to see some action. From thirty rows up, she screamed, "Stop P-word-footing around!"

P-word-footing?

Stop pussyfooting around—that's certainly what she meant.

"Stop P-word-footing around!" she screamed again. And then, only a skosh more quietly, as she'd had perhaps a beer or seventeen, she turned to explain to a companion, "I don't use the fucking P-word."

I saw that night not only the crowning of the new lightweight boxing champion of the world, but perhaps the crowning of the new lightweight mis-etymological champion of the world, as well.

Pussyfoot is not a bad word, even though it is generally used derisively. To pussyfoot is to tread carefully, as on little kittycat paws.

By the by, I didn't bother trying to define the word for this vocal boxing fan, nor did I point out to her that, by the by, the F-wording F-word *is* bad. It still boggles. Won't say *pussyfoot*. Will say *fuck*. I shake my head.

HOGWASH

My etymology of *hogwash* is not . . . oh, you know where I'm leading . . .

What's the source of the word *hogwash*? Cleaning pigs? Spraying them down? Giving them a nice bubble bath and perhaps a pedicure (would that be a hooficure?)

Hogwash!

The *wash* in *hogwash* is what is washed out—in this sense, washed out of kitchens or other places of consumable preparation, including breweries (in other words, garbage and scraps and such), and fed to the hogs. By the 1700s, the term was used to describe any hog-sloppy liquor, and extended to other sorts of inferior things (such as this book, some of you are thinking). The word took further figurative use to eventually become synonymous with slang *baloney!,* which comes from *balogna,* which is usually made from, um . . . hogs well-washed (hopefully in both senses of the word).

OINK OINK

George Orwell, E.B. White, and Chuck Jones aside, pigs do not speak English.

Well, pigs didn't speak English before the 1930s, apparently, when use of the word *oink* was first recorded. Other animals seem to be much more literate. Cows have been mooing and cats have been meowing for many centuries, since at least the 1500s and the 1600s, respectively, in English. Cows and cats are, in fact, multilingual, as they've been mooing and meowing (cows and cats—don't confuse the order) in other languages for thousands of years. And dogs?—they've been bow-wowing in English since the 1500s, as well. In fact, they were quite literate in doing so, as Shakespeare himself quotes them in *The Tempest*: "Harke, harke, bowgh wawgh: the watch-Dogges barke."

But the pigs have been slow to pick up their own English words. I've asked why, but they respond with the recent acronym OINK (*honest! I read it on the Internet!*), which stands for "Oh I've No Komment," proving that pigs can't spell English, either.

SWINE
The Latin name for pig is not *sweetswineomine*.

English is blessed with multiple levels of formality and nuance for many of its synonymous words, resulting from English's many and continued influences from other languages. A classic example is *ask/question/interrogate*, with the blunt *ask* from the foundation of Anglo-Saxon (Old English); the slightly stiffer *question* (fourteenth century) from the Anglo-French period, and the formal *interrogate* (fifteenth century) introduced from Latin.

This is why we have such Anglo-Saxon/Latin functional/scientific synonym combinations as *bear/ursine, cat/feline, cow/bovine, hound/canine, fish/piscine, fox/vulpine, horse/equine, omydarlin/clementine, pig/swine, sheep/ovine, weasel/musteline* (use *that* as a conversation-starter at your next party), *wolf/lupine* . . .

Hold on there, Porky. All that sounded good, but that's not all, folks. *Cat* and *cow* and *hound* are indeed Anglo-Saxon, as are the others, including . . . *swine*. Not *pig*. The Anglo-Saxon progression above should really be *swine/porcine*. We're not sure where the word *pig* came from, and though it shows up in Chaucer, it wasn't particularly common until the 1800s. (Nor, for that matter, do we know where the word *dog* came from, as *hound* was the common term coming out of Old English. And we absolutely know where the word *omydarlin* comes from, and stop pointing fingers at me.)

COWARD
File under "Herd, Cow and Shep": There is no *cow* in *coward*.

A number of insulting words have been grown in rustic and agricultural settings, including *villain* (originally the worker who tended the lands of a villa). Despite the occasional speculation that it is pejorative reference to the hard-working cowherd, *coward* is not among these words. Fueling the speculation that *coward* resulted from the likely swallowing of the *h* in *cowherd* is the way we pronounce "sheperd" for the sheep-herder. But there is no *cow* in *coward*. Unless it is refers to a frightened heifer turning tail.

The key word in *coward* is actually French: *coue,* meaning "tail." The insulting word *coward* pins a tail on the tail by adding the suffix *-ard,* in a word-formation similar to other insults like *dullard, sluggard* and *drunkard.* Our coward, therefore, is someone who displays his tail by having turned it and tucked it tenaciously between his legs.

And what of a sentence like "The coward cowherd cowered"? Delightful coincidence, and nothing more. *Cower* is likely of Scandinavian origin, and originally had neutral meanings of squatting or bending over.

Also of likely Scandinavian origin is another word that our frightened heifer can take heart in, though, again, it is unrelated to the other similar sounds in this discussion. *To cow* is to intimidate. So, young heifer, turn around and stand up to your herder. You're bigger than he is. Cow, cow the coward cowherd!

GREYHOUND

Greyhounds are not grey.

Well, some greyhounds are grey. But others are befurred in other colors, yet aren't called blackhounds, brownhounds, tan-and-white-hounds, greasy-rolled-in-the-neighbors'-garbage-hounds, or silver-hounds-with-glass-windows-and-windshield-wipers (oh, sorry,

those are the busses). The second syllable in *greyhound* is the venerable English word meaning "dog," but the first syllable is not
related to our word for somewhere-between-black-and-white. *Grey*
is likely related, way back from Old English times, to the Old Norse
word *griey*, meaning "bitch." Therefore, "female hound" (in the
technical and not the pejorative use of the word *bitch*). Another definition for *griey* seems to be "coward." Therefore, "coward hound."
And a pretty successful coward hound, at that—one that can run
away real fast, making greyhounds the canine version of scaredy-
cats.

And, oh yeah, if you need me to explain that bloodhounds aren't
the color of blood, I suggest that perhaps you should stay away from
the pooches and get yourself a pet rock.

Abecedarianisms

This portion of *Everything You Know About English Is Wrong* is a love letter to letters. You can sing letters in the ABC song, you can twist them in different typefaces, you can rearrange them endlessly and create these things called words, with nuance of choice (for example, see the entry for "*Gray/Grey*" on page 191 in this section).

Not everyone loves specific letters. In 1779, Benjamin Franklin published his *A Scheme for a New Alphabet and a Reformed Mode of Spelling*, which proposed to eliminate *C, J, Q, W, X,* and *Y*. Those letters, Franklin noted, kould be replased uith ekzisting karakters. I, being a suspicious sort, am deeply concerned that this proposal was shot down for political reasons; the *Scrabble* lobby was very strong, even then. Franklin proposed six new characters, including "ish" to handle the *sh* sound. He also suggested a new alphabetical order, which would have to have been renamed "oh-oh-atical order," as he proposed *O* become the first letter, followed by a new character, *oa* (in ligature and pronounced as the *O* in "John").[60]

Ambrose Bierce expressed his chagrin over a couple of letters in his *Devil's Dictionary*, including this grousing (or should I say, *growsing*):

> W (double U) has, of all the letters in our alphabet, the only cumbrous name, the names of the others being monosyllabic. This advantage of the Roman alphabet over the Grecian is the more valued after audibly spelling out some simple Greek word, like epixoriambikos. Still, it is now thought by the learned that other agencies than the difference of the two alphabets may have been concerned in the decline of "the glory that was Greece" and the rise of "the grandeur that was Rome." There can

---

[60] It should be duly noted that Franklin's proposal, in modern parlance, never made it past alpha version into beta testing.

be no doubt, however, that by simplifying the name of W (calling it "wow," for example) our civilization could be, if not promoted, at least better endured.

Supporting Bierce's suggestion is the fact that, interestingly, the symbol that is the parent of *W* so many centuries back is the Phoenician letter called "wau."

Now, with Ambrose as our inspiration, let's engage in a bit of orthography, my favorite big word meaning "spelling": Using his suggested letter name, we would spell the word *wow* as *Wow O Wow!* And how would you spell the spelling? "*Wow oh wow oh wow oh wow*" . . . which sounds positively orthogasmic.

And besides, I as a language lover find poetic beauty in understanding that every *word* begins with a *wow*.

But back to Mr. Franklin's proposal. He designed his updated alphabet to begin with *O* and end in *M,* which is somehow appropriate to this discussion, as we will start by pointing out that the final letter of the current alphabet is not the last, and end by pointing out that the first letter of the current alphabet is not the first.

Z

The last letter of the alphabet is not Z.

Z is not the final letter of the alphabet for several reasons.

The first is technical: Allow me to restate the headline of this note as an American would say it. "The last letter of the alphabet is not *Zee.*" And our sample American would be right, because *zed* is the last letter of the alphabet. In the States, the letter is referred to as "*zee*"; for the rest of the English-speaking world, it's referred to as *zed*.

Nothing wrong with this difference. It's not going to cause any sort of international misunderstanding ("You mean Zimbabwe with a *zee?* We sent the Prime Minister to Zimbabwe with a *zed!*"). And no one is going to attempt to get the States in synch with the rest of the world (witness the success in converting the U.S. to the metric system). Just thought you'd like to know.

The second reason *Z* is not the last letter of the alphabet is historical: *Z* should not be the last letter of the alphabet. While the alphabet has changed considerably in its evolution from Phoenician through Greek through Etruscan through Latin, the order of the letters largely has not. Call it *alep* or *aleph* or *alpha* or *a,* the alphabet starts with *a.* Learn your *alep-bayit-gimels;* your *aleph-beth-gimels;* your *alpha-beta-gammas;* your *ABCs.* But when the Romans adapted the Etruscan alphabet, they eliminated *Z,* which had been the seventh letter of the Phoenician alphabet and the eighth letter of the Greek ("I am the Alpha and the Omega," not "I am the Alpha and the Zeta"). When the Romans reintroduced *Z,* its place had been taken. No cuts! To the end of the line with you!

The third reason *Z* is not the last letter of the alphabet is likewise historical. And here we're talking about the last to be added, because five—count 'em—five letters were added to our alphabet even after *Z*'s triumphal return. The Latin alphabet when introduced to the Anglo-Saxons failed to represent three sounds used by the native peoples. Two sounds were very close to our present-day *th lithp* sound, and the native letters representing them are þ and Ð, thorn and eth. A third was wynn (the *W* sound, represented by the still-surviving letter *W* (which literally began as VV).[61] When the letters *J* and *V* came along, they, like the later *W,* got their cuts into the middle of the line, because, in a sense, they had connections. *I* snuck *J* in (because *I* needed a break, having functioned to

---

[61] Literally in the literal sense of *literal.* See page 157 for more information.

communicate both the *I* and *J* sounds), and *U* snuck *V* in (it, too, need an assistant after all that time representing both the *U* and *V* sounds).

Is it unfair that these letters, particularly *V* and *W,* got cuts? Sure, but after all, it's all about who U know.

YE

File under "O Ye of Little Faith": There is no such word as *Ye* in phrases like "Ye Olde."

You have perhaps seen the sign for that quaint retail establishment, "Ye Olde þornography Shoppe" (well, maybe not as often as I have). There are lies and there are truths in that sign, and let's untangle them.

First of all, despite appearances, the primary word is not *Pornography*. The first letter in that word is actually a now-obsolete Old English letter, "þ," which indicated the "th" sound. So our retail establishment is actually "The Olde Thornography Shoppe," appropriate because the name of the letter þ is thorn.

And you've likely noticed that I also changed *Ye* to *The* when I clarified the shop's name. Specifically, it should be "þe Olde Thornography Shoppe," because there is no *Y* in the first word. When thorn was handwritten, it was often mistaken for *Y,* and when typesetting came along, *Y* was often used to indicate the disappearing thorn character when setting ye olde manuscrippes. Thus the word *the,* written as þe, was misinterpreted as *Ye.*

However, the ultimate lie in my example is that to my knowledge there is no retail establishment called "Olde Pornography Shoppe," and don't you *dare* put this book down to go find out.[62]

---

[62] But send me the address when you find it.

U

It's not always about U.

As I write this, Sue Grafton has mysteried her way through most of the alphabet with her remarkable series of abecedarian whodunits, starting with *A Is for Alibi* and *B Is for Burglar,* and so on (I believe that something related to *C* was next). The series has successfully progressed to its latest volume, *T Is for Trespass.* What's next?

I can guarantee you that Grafton's next book will *not* be *U Is for Victim.*

Though it could be. And properly so, at least in a historical sense.

The letter *V* is a relative newcomer to the English alphabet. Now, the "vee" sound has been with us for a long time, as has the "you" sound, but these sounds were represented by a single letter—*U.* Like *Y, U* could be both consonant and vowel, as could the letter *I* (also see "Vowels, Part IV (and I mean the alphabet letters, not the Roman Numerals)" on page 192 for more on that.) The Romans used *V* to represent sounds that we communicate with *U, V,* and *W.* In fact, *W,* another johnny-come-letterly, is literally double-*U,* with the *U* looking like *V*—squinch 'em together: *VV.* (If the idea of *V* having multiple functions like that seems odd to you, consider a couple of things we accept every day, though when we look at them closely, they seem a little bizarre: hard-*C,* soft-*C;* hard-*G,* soft-*G.*)

This multiple use contributed to why we have what seems to be complete dyslexia in this quote from Robert Cawdrey's pioneering dictionary, *A Table Alphabeticall* (1604): "Do we not speak, because we would haue other to vnderstand vs? or is not the tongue giuen

for this end, that one might know what another meaneth?" Hauing
others to vndersand vs is a noble goal indeed, which is why I'm also
amused by the unintentional irony of this quote from Henry
Cockeram's *The English dictionarie, or an interpreter of hard English
words* (1623): "Vacillate, to wauer, to be inconstant." Nothing like a
wauering letter to keep vs all confused.[63]

QOPH

File under, "Q, A Barrel Full of": In English spelling, *U* does
not have to follow *Q*.

One of my favorite words is *queue*. This word is the quintessential
expression of an English spelling rule so dominant we'll call a
dominatrix rule: "*U* must follow *Q*! Slave!" The letter *Q* in *queue* is
obediently followed by *two U*'s, though not in close proximity lest
they handcuff themselves to each other and become *W*.

The *Q-U* spelling rule is so stringent that even looking hard, you
find few exceptions. What's more, those you do find are archaisms,
borrowings from other languages, or proper names. Sure, fly Qantas.[64]
Visit lovely Iraq. Email me a nasty letter from your Compaq.

But my favorite word that does *not* exhibit the *Q-U* combination
is one that's accepted by the ultimate word authority—not by the
Oxford English Dictionary, not by the French *Academie Francais*,
which doesn't control English but very likely would like to, but by
The Official Scrabble Players Dictionary.

The word is *qoph*. Letters in the Phoenician alphabet denoted
animals and everyday things; for instance, *aleph* ("ox"), *mem*
("water") and *zayin* ("weapon"). *Qoph* represented "monkey" (and

---

[63] V was used (vsed) to begin words, and U internally, leading to the Latin word *uva* being
written *vua*, as pointed out by Ron Koster.

[64] I'm shocked that this airline hasn't come out with a campaign saying, "We respect our
customers so much, we changed our name, and put U in Quantas." (On the other hand, I'm
a smart-aleck language observer and not a copywriter, which is why other folks get the big
writing bucks. Revise: which is why other folks get any bucks at all.)

not monquey). Qoph the monkey (Creationist-inclined folks, avert your eyes for a second) evolved from its Phoenician origins through Greek and Latin and etc. and etc. into the modern entity it is today: standing tall, and alone, as . . . our letter *Q*.

LETTERS

File under "Dotting your *T*'s and crossing your eyes": The cliché "Make sure to dot your *I*'s and cross your *T*'s" doesn't go nearly far enough.

Make sure you dot your *J*'s, too.

And cross your *D*'s. Wait. You don't have to do that anymore.

A crossed *D* was an Old English character called eth—Đ— which indicated the "th" sound, as did sister character thorn (see page 184). But like thorn, eth is obsolete. Though it's redundant to say in its visually punnish way, it has seen its Đeth.[65]

GRAY/GREY

File under "Graeying": When it comes to meaning, *gray* is not quite gray enough.

"*Grey* in the U.K. and *gray* in the U.S.A." seems to be the rule of two accepted spelling variants, but the differences run a bit deeper than that. The variant spellings so noted are each more common on their respective sides of the pond, granted, but a strong bit of nuance over nationality is at play. Though I'm hardly the first to point out the difference in nuance (nuence?), I agree that *grey* is greyer than

---

[65] Good name for a heavy metal band, isn't it?

gray. Look at the flattened *e,* almost sighing in contrast to the fuller, prouder *a.*

Which is why, though I accept growing gray, I rail against growing grey.

ET CETERA, ETC., AND SO ON AND SO FORTH AND BLAH BLAH BLAH.

&c. is not an abomination (well, other than the fact that you could stop using what it stands for in the first place).

&c. is not an abomination? Well, yes it is, but not just for the reason you're probably applying to it. Yes, it's confusing (*ampersand-c? huh?*—it means "etc."). And it's plain ol' ugly.

But what it's not is this: It is not a cute insertion of the ampersand (&) into the tried abbreviation etc. In a sense, etc. *created* ampersand.

The "and" symbol is not a fancifully written script version of the plus sign. It is technically a ligature—the combination of two letters or characters. The U.S. dollar sign is a ligature, as is an Old English vowel now retired: Æ (ash—see the next entry for more info). The ampersand combines the letters *E* and *T,* spelling *et,* Latin meaning "and," the *et* in *et cetera.*

VOWELS, PART I

File under "Ash to Ashes, Dust to Dust": *A, E, I, O, U,* and sometimes *Y* are not the only English vowel letters.

Name the Beatles. Paul McCartney, John Lennon, George Harrison, Ringo Starr, and sometimes session man Billy Preston. But many of us remember, as well we should, that there was another Beatle—original drummer Pete Best.

The musical-language group The Vowel Vocal Band has a similar oft-forgotten drummer. In addition to the core group members *A, E, I, O, U,* and occasional session vowel *Y* is a Pete-Best vowel known as "ash." Ash was one of a few runic symbols added to the Roman alphabet, used by Latin-literate priests transcribing Old English. Because transcriptions at the time were done phonetically (a "primitive" practice that we have since largely abandoned), and because Englisc speakers used sounds not represented in the Roman alphabet, the occasional rune was employed to communicate those sounds. Ash is pronounced like the *A* in its name, and is represented by the symbol *Æ*. The word *ash* has also been spelled *æsc* and *asc,* which confuses me a bit: I don't understand why the vowel's name wasn't *always* spelled *æsh*. Surely all the Old English keyboards had the symbol.

The letter ash bit the dust sometime during the Middle English period, leaving us with a simple *A* to do its former work.

Now, bringing the discussion back to the moptop mania that began this little essay, I must note that in the very early days of the Beatles, when Pete Best was still the drummer, the group called themselves the Quarrymen, and for a time before assuming the name we know them by now, they called themselves (yes, it's almost true, and you'll see it in a bullshitternet post soon) . . . the *Bætles*.

"I wænnæ hold your hænd!"

VOWELS, PART II

File under "Play, Vowel": English vowels are not only *A, E, I, O, U,* and *sometimes Y—again.*

One of my grade-school teachers once bet our class five dollars that we couldn't find a word that lacked a vowel. Every English word, we were instructed, must have a vowel—*A, E, I, O, U,* and sometimes *Y,* in the classic listing. Now, five bucks was a lot of money at the time, so we mulled and tested and poked at this theory for . . . well, for about ten minutes because recess was coming up and we had a lot of jungle-gymming to do.

I wish I could remember which teacher that was, because, as you can imagine, my jungle-gym mastery has declined considerably over the years and I've therefore been able to devote some time to locating some English words that I offer as exhibiting vowelless-ness. I don't seek to show up my esteemed grade-school teacher; I simply need the five-spot for a gallon of gas.

My first candidate was a word I encountered some years after the challenge. *Cwm* is a geological term, synonymous with *cirque*—a hollow ground out by glacial action. *Cwm* is of Welsh origin, and was in use by the 1850s (which is *not* when I was in grade school, thank you very much). So, then, *A, E, I, O, U,* and sometimes *Y* and *W.*

Then I thought about words like *grr*—an onomatopoeic inter-jection indicating anger (or better yet, angerrr). *Grr* is a word by my estimation (and it's the basis of one of my favorite neologisms: *grrl,* meaning an angrry woman). And now we stand at *A, E, I, O, U,* and sometimes *Y, W,* and *R.*

Then, with dreams of my billfold bulging with fivers, I thought to offer acronyms and initialisms. "The description fits you to a T!"

T is a word, and if it has a vowel, it must be the *T*. Now our list stands at *A, E, I, O, U,* and sometimes *Y, W, R,* and *T*.

So, have I convinced you that some English words lack vowels? Good. Because now you're wrong, as I'll explain in the next entry. You can keep the five.

VOWELS, PART III
Five vowels, traditionally, maybe six? Nah. Maybe dozens.

The saga of "English vowels are not necessarily *A, E, I, O, U,* and sometimes *Y*" continues.

Most of us have learned that *A, E, I, O, U,* and sometimes *Y* are vowels, and specific to that precise classification I offer no argument (with the exception, of course, of the waggish additions in the entries above and below). However, as I tick off the letter list in the previous sentence, I count 1, 2, 3, 4, 5, and sometimes 6 vowels . . . even though when talking about vowels, there are actually in the range of 14, 15, 16 . . .

Specifically, the components of our oft-detailed list above are vowel *letters,* vowel *symbols,* used to record and express vowel *sounds,* and in fact the word *vowel* was used to denote the sound (as early as the 1300s) before being applied to the letter (in the 1500s). *Vowel* comes from Old French *vouel* (single *u* instead of double-*u*, and so much truer to the spirit of the word, though I find it fascinating that one English spelling of *vowel* was *wowell*). Old French *vouel* in turn traces back to Latin *vocal,* and meaning a sound produced with the vocal cords (as opposed to consonant sounds, produced by bursts of air controlled by lip, tongue, etc.). So a single vowel (letter) has multiple personalities—for instance, the letter *A* does a Sybil to become long-*A made*, short-*A had*, schwa-*A ma*, and then teams up with other letters to create, for instance, the sound in *haughty*.

But even if we stick to limiting our discussion to symbols as vowels, the *AEIOU/Y* rule is not strictly true today. More accurately, perhaps, "The vowels are *A, I, O, U*, and sometimes *E* and *Y*." In the original sense of the word *vowel*, the letter *E* in the word *made* is not a vowel at all—unvocalized, it loses its true vowel status. Granted, the *E* does work as an indicator of how the *A* should be pronounced, but once upon an Old English/Middle English time, that *E* would have been pronounced. (We could begin to question the permanent vowel status of the other letters by digging into their activities—we're keeping our eye on *I*, as in the word *parliament*— but this book has only so many pages.) So these days the letter *E* pretends to vowel tenure by clinging to its technical classification as a letter. I suspect it's trying to retain its pension.

VOWELS, PART IV (AND I MEAN THE ALPHABET LETTERS, NOT THE ROMAN NUMERALS)

See the preceding "Vowels" subheads, rinse, and repeat.

To complete this little roundelay of vowel play, let's first recap where we are. In Parts I and III, we concluded that our tongue-in-cheek list of vowels now stands at *A, I, O, U*, and sometimes *E, Y, W*, and *R*.

Now, see my entry for the letter *Z* on page 182, in which I point out that the letters *I* and *U* were also used as consonants before complementary *J* and *V* were introduced to the alphabet. And in fact *V* and *U* were somewhat interchangeable, as were *I* and *J*, given the circumstance: Consider *IVLIVS*, which is not a Roman numeral, but an English spelling of *Julius*. *U* and *V* were kind of like UV light—visible only under certain conditions. Then add in the fact that double-u was formed literally as two joined *U* or *V* characters, and we're forced to revise the lineup even further: *A* and *O*, and sometimes *E, I, J, U, V, W, R, T, Y* (starting to look like a keyboard row, isn't it?), and once-upon a time *Æ*.

For that matter, if we get real technical and decide to finally add in *A* and *O* as sometimes vowels because they also act as words, well, we have no pure vowels left at all.

I feel like I've just completed the linguistic murder version of Agatha Christie's *Ten Little Indians*.

ME, MYSELFS, AND I
A is not the first letter of the alphabet.

Despite the fact that dictionaries, encyclopedias, and English-class roll call all start with *A*-words for alphabetical order, despite the fact that the word *alphabetical* itself starts with the letter *A*, for philosophical and not language-history reasons, there is a letter of far greater primary importance to communication in English. For an explanation, I yield the floor to one Mr. Ambrose Bierce, from his *The Devil's Dictionary*:

> 'I' is the first letter of the alphabet, the first word of the language, the first thought of the mind, the first object of affection. . . . The frank yet graceful use of 'I'

distinguishes a good writer from a bad; the latter carries
it with the manner of a thief trying to cloak his loot.

So, of course, Mr. Franklin's modest proposal notwithstanding,
A is the first letter of the alphabet, the first letter of the word
alphabet, the first letter of a series of Sue Grafton mysteries, the first
. . . well, you get my point. I concede. To do otherwise would be to
carry my first tongue-in-cheek claim with the manner of Mr.
Bierce's thief.

Making Fun, Having Fun

Following, a few words and thoughts I'm fond of, and will make fun of, while having fun. If you *fun* someone in the original sense of the word, you make him or her a fool. That person is funned, foolish—source of our word *fond.*

I've made the above point elsewhere, but I still have fun doing it so I'll do it again for these pages. Besides, it makes a more interesting introduction than just calling it "Miscellaneous" and saying "Here's some more crap you didn't know about."

But, what the hell. Here's some more crap you didn't know about:

KNIGHT

File under "Knights, K-Nasty, Run Away!": The English do not speak better English than the French.

Well, at least better than one Frenchman, who happens to be English. I'll explain:

In a classic scene (among so many classic scenes) in *Monty Python and the Holy Grail,* John Cleese portrays an obnoxious French castle guard taunting King Arthur and his knights. Among his many derisions, the French guard refers to the lot of them as "silly English k-nig-its." On the surface, the joke is that this rude guard (and likely part-time waiter) doesn't know that the English word *knight* features silent consonants, or is mocking Arthur with mispronunciation. But if we consider it a bit more deeply, we see that the joke that Messrs. Cleese and his fellow Pythons may or may not have considered is that some French consonants can themselves be silent, so it would seem unlikely that the guard would go out of his way to pronounce every single English letter (yes, it's a joke for word geeks like me, and you can berate me for it—on the other hand, *you* are still reading this book).

The better word-geek joke, though—again, one that Cleese and company may or may not have realized—is that the Frenchman was pretty close to being right (or rig-git).

Arthur is said to have lived in the fifth century, when Old English was spoken. The Old English word that eventually became *knight* in modern English was *cniht* (synonymous with *lad*), in which the hard-*C* was pronounced. This word was synonymous with other West Germanic language words, such as *knecht* in Old Frisian, Middle Dutch, and German. And when Chaucer was writing, in Middle English, *knight* was pronounced *ka-nick-te* (though unlikely spoken by the French guard, who would have been very old by Chaucer's time). *Knight,* along with other silent-*K* words like *knee* and *knock* and *knot* and *know* and *knuckle*, retained the hard-*C* pronunciation even after Shakespeare's time, and started going silent in the sixteenth century even though related words in other Germanic languages retain the *K-N* dual sound.

I'm not sure of the verisimilitude of the other Frenchman's taunts in *Holy Grail,* including "Your mother was a hamster and your father smelt of elderberries!," but given the delightful erudition of the French guard's understanding of Old English elocution, I now believe this movie to be a study in meticulous adherence to historical veracity—especially the catapulting of cows from within the walls of French castles.

CENTER/CENTRE, THEATER/THEATRE

File under "Centre of the Univrese, The": *Theatre* and *centre* were not always the British spellings.

The meaning, usage, and spelling of English words vary from country to country, from region to region, from street to street, or so it sometimes seems. We could spend the next eighty-five pages chronicling the differences among American, Canadian, British, Australian, Caribbean, and other Englishes, and in fact in my first draft I did just that, but the editor cut them out and made me write some original stuff, darn him.

One difference between American and British English intrigues me, though. If British writers insist on the spellings of *theatre* and *centre,* why don't these self-same communicators refer to themselves as writres?

I know, I know—that's just being cute. There are technical reasons for this variance. *Theater* and *center* come to us through French and ultimately from Latin *theatrum* and *centrum,* while *writer* is a core Old English word, using the standard *-er* suffix on the verb *write.* Word function plays into the difference, as well. After all (aftre all?), a theater is not one who theates, and a center is not one who cents.

But here's the interesting part: Before the publication of Samuel Johnson's *A Dictionary of the English Language,* a major factor in solidifying spelling when it was published in 1755, the words in question were commonly spelled *theater* and *center.* And among those who used those spellings? A certain Mr. William Shakespeare, and if *Shakespeare* wants to spell *theater* that way, far be it for me to argue. (He was a hell of a writre, aftre all.)

TEAM
There is no truth to the idea that there is no *I* in team.

It's one of the standard motivational clichés. "There is no *I* in *team*." *Rally rally, yawn yawn, buy my motivational tapes!* (If we want to play that game, there is also no *I* in *ego*. And just to be contentious, though there's no *I* in *team*, there *is* a mixed-up *ME* in the word.)

However, Mr. Motivational Speaker, there used to be an *I* in *team*, back in the 1600s when it was spelled, though probably not frequently, as *taime*. Back when the *me* in *team* wasn't quite so mixed up.[66]

CELSIUS, COOL REGARD FOR
In a linguistically just world, the alternative to the Fahrenheit Scale is not the Celsius Scale.

We Americans measure temperature in degrees Fahrenheit. On this scale, water freezes at 32 degrees and boils at 212 degrees, and though there's method to these seemingly arbitrary numbers, I shall bore neither you nor myself by repeating that method here. The rest of the world has moved to measuring in degrees Celsius. In this system, water freezes at 0 degrees and boils at 100 (although when Mr. Anders Celsius invented the scale in 1742, he designated 0 as the boiling point and 100 for the freezing point—more on that in a moment). The Celsius scale employs a tidy metric scheme—for example, 50 degrees is halfway between freezing and boiling, while in Fahrenheit, 50 degrees is . . . well . . . hotter than 32.

To convert a Fahrenheit measurement into Celsius (bear with me), one employs this formula: $°C = (°F - 32) \times (5 \div 9)$, and using your fingers and toes isn't allowed.

---

[66]There is also no *I* in the phrase "The author of the book before you," but here I am nonetheless.

So what the hell does this have to do with English? This: where *Celsius* effectively employs mathematical meter, it stomps all over literary meter. I'm certain Mr. Celsius was a fine gent, but his name has all the pronounceability of *she sells Celsius down by the seashore.* Frustrating, considering that the scale used to be called the Centigrade Scale.

Centigrade—literally, 100 degrees—is a marvelous match of form and content, a precise metric word for a precise metric measurement. But in 1948, the *Conférence générale des poids et mesures* and the *Comité international des poids et measures* decided to honor Mr. Celsius by taking the word *centigrade,* dividing it by 2, multiplying it by *shhhhh,* and destroying some exquisite linguistic and mathematical correlation.

Now, in 1744, the year of Celsius's death, a botanist using a centigrade thermometer decided to swap the meaning of 0 and 100 on the scale, so that rising numbers more logically denoted rising heat. If only this gentleman had been around in 1948 to overturn the regrettable naming decision of the *Conférence générale des poids et masures à raconter des bêtises,* turning the new name of the scale completely upside-down to its more logical elocution, just as he had the scale itself. And he would have had the power to do it, this Mr. Carolus Linnaeus, pioneer of formal, studied, logical taxonomical nomenclature that we use today.[67]

SONG LYRICS
File under "The Book of Love, Whom Wrote, Me Wonders Wonders Wonders": I can't get no satisfaction neither.

---

[67] But even now I need to backtrack, as "Carolus Linnaeus" is the Latinized version of "Carl von Linne," a version resulting from Carl naming himself with Latin influence since he wrote scientific tracts in Latin. Had he followed Scandinavian tradition, Carl who lived in Linne would have been Carl Nilsson (as his father's name was Nils). Carolus Linnaeus is oddly the Celsius-ized version of the name. By the way, it was Carl's innovation that gave us such taxonomical designations as Homo sapiens for humans, Orycteropus afer for aardvarks, and Artemisia tilesii for stinkweed. Because Carl had the power to name every living thing on the planet, I'll concede him the right to name himself.

Steven Pinker, in his readable, edifying, essential *The Language Instinct: How the Mind Creates Language*, takes to task the nonsense that the word *their* can't be used with perceived singular nouns with this comment: "Everyone returned to his seat makes it sound like Bruce Springsteen was discovered during intermission to be in the audience, and everyone rushed back and converged on his seat to await an autograph."

Everyone will await his autograph, but not his grammar advice. Why should they, since the Boss wrote such ungrammatical lyrics as "Nowhere to run ain't got nowhere to go" and "Ain't nobody likes to be alone." Heck, Mr. Springstien can't even spell his own name right.

But I'm not here to engage in persnickitation about grammar in song lyrics. I'm here to cheer appropriate bad grammar in song. I'm both amused and dumbfounded by the occasional web arguments about ungrammatical song lyrics, pointing out that Bob Dylan's "Lay Lady Lay" should really be "Lie Lady Lie" or that Eric Clapton shouldn't be singing "Lay Down Sally" when the lyric really should be "Lie Down Sally." (Hey—maybe the song is being addressed to someone who has thrown Sally over his shoulder. "Lay down Sally! Put the Sally down, and step away from the Sally!")

We see deep, meaningful insight in such lyricritical arguments, such as the web post that decried the Creedence Clearwater Revival lyric "if I was a bricklayer" from the song "Penthouse Pauper," by saying, "It's 'if I were'! Dumbass!'" And I'm not making the "Dumbass" reference up. (Oddly, after a stanza if "if I was" lyrics, Creedence songwriter/singer John Fogerty switches to two stanzas of "if I were" lyrics, the smartass, and then a final stanza that contains both "if I were" and "if I was" lyrics, the dumbass.)

Myself, my favorite bit of grammar gymnastics comes in "Horse With No Name," the '70s megahit from the band America. One lyric explains that the loneliness of the desert allows you the facility to remember your own name, because in such an expanse "there ain't no one for to give you no pain." To me, that begs the questions: Would you forget your name if there *was* someone for to give you no pain? (Or, if there *were*—dumbass!?) And would you remember or forget your name if there were someone for to give you *some* pain? And does anybody remember what we were even talking about a moment ago?

We were talking about grammar in song lyrics, and how the language is scarred by otherwise eloquent headbangers misusing the mother tongue in popular music. Ultimately, who cares?

Well, I care. And I say, force the songwriters and singers to adhere to the truth of linguistics. Darnit!

But the truth of linguistics in the case of song lyrics and other artistic presentations is not grammar, but vernacular. The people who would have Mick Jagger singing "(I Can Achieve Nary a Modicum of) Propitiation" ("hey hey hey, that's what I orate") ignore the fact that, other than the old *Schoolhouse Rock* lessons on Saturday-morning kids' TV, popular music isn't here to edify. It exists to tell stories. Stories have narrators and narrators have voice—a way of speaking, a style of storytelling. "I can't get no girlie action" is voice. Force grammar into the characters of stories, and you'll have Nicely Nicely singing "When you see a gentleman reach for stars in the firmament" in the next revival of the Damon-Runyon-based musical, *Guys and Dolls*.

So I say, go ahead, lady, lay across the big brass bed. Meantime, I'll be listening to one of my favorite bands, Pete Townsend and The Whom. I like The Whom and their songs. Yes. *Their* songs. Crank up the album *Whom's Next*, Mr. Pinker!

VEGETARIAN

T-Shirts do not always speak the truth. (And this comes as a surprise?)

Here's a T-shirt I saw some time ago: "*Vegetarian*—an old word for 'bad hunter.'" Ah, so ridiculously etymologically incorrect, of course, for the purpose of a clever line. Just thought you'd like to know. (File under "bullshitTshirtnet" instead of "bullshitternet.")

This set me to wondering why the back-when vegetarians didn't adopt the technical term for one who eats only plants: *herbivore*. Did the technical nature, particularly with beasty implications, affect the decision? The words *herbivore* and *carnivore* do imply animals, not people.

Was it the desire to create a memorable "statement" word? After all, *vegetarian* is relatively new, first recorded in 1839 and likely popularized by the creation of the Vegetarian Society in England in 1847.

Or was it the fact that the word *herbivore* may not have existed in 1839—in English, anyway? The word is derived from a 1748 French manuscript, but isn't recorded in English until 1854.

So let's revise the T-shirt: "*Herbivore*—a slightly less old word for 'bad hunter.'"

SCRABBLE

File under "AAAQOWJIFLQWIUZZZJRHA": Scrabble is not playing fair.

A venerable and duly venerated game is *Scrabble*, the crossword board game that awards you for creating big words with little-used letters inscribed on tiles that you place strategically, orthographically, and carefully (those darned tiles are slippery) on a game board. If any of this is news to you, I shake my head about why you would be reading a book about language.

I love playing *Scrabble*, but I've been losing a lot lately because I've been adhering to the intent of the game's name—in its historical sense, that is. *Scrabble* burst on the commercial scene in the 1950s, even though it was invented in 1933 and wasn't marketed until a couple of decades later. The July 20, 1953, edition of *Time*, discussing the *Scrabble* phenomenon, wrote this: "In 1948 a social worker named James Brunot took it over and invented the name 'scrabble' (dictionary meaning: 'to scrape, paw or scratch with the hands or feet')."

Allow me to make a couple of points here (as if you had any way of stopping me other than shutting this book):

1) Inventing a word that already exists is a prodigious feat indeed.

2) Brunot would have been more credible had he spelled his name *Bruneaux* and signed that contract not on the dotted line but over a triple word score.

3) Most important, the 1953 dictionaries were apparently pretty limited, because today's online edition of the *Oxford*

English Dictionary informs me that one of the first meanings of the verb *to scrabble,* from the 1500s, is "To make marks at random."

So if *to scrabble* is "to make marks at random," how can my fellow *Scrabble* players possibly disallow such eloquent randomly marked words as *AAAQOWJIFLQWIUZZZJRHA?*

It's just not fair.[68, 69]

PIG-ASS

Pig-ass and *pig-wife* are not insults (snicker snicker).

Sure sure sure, the words *pig-ass* and *pig-wife* sound like offshoots of that faddish collection of "yo mama is so fat" jokes ("yo wife is so pig . . ."). But here the word *pig* means a type of earthenware container. A pig-wife sold those containers (compare *fishwife,* a female fish vendor[70]), and a pig-ass was the donkey that hauled them around. Note: These words are spoken by a professional on a closed course. Do not try them at home, because you'll get walloped before you get a chance to blurt out even the first few words of their real meaning.

GREASE

Grease is not the word, not the word, not the word.

Some years ago, *Sesame Street,* the PBS educational kids show, decided to stage a musical. The theatrical extravaganza of choice was the Rodgers and Hammerstein classic *Oklahoma!* The morning I watched was O what a beautiful morning. The corn was as high

---

[68] (Which is what the word *AAAQOWJIFLQWIUZZZJRHA* means: "It's just not fair.")

[69] I once won a Scrabble tournament by using my 8,000-point tiles for the Old English letters thorn and eth. The officials quickly recognized my counterfeiting, but nonetheless awarded me first place for my ingenuity, and of course all that is a lie.

[70] Interestingly, *fishwife* has been used pejoratively more often than *pig-wife,* though this footnote is in no way seeking to balance things by pointing out the possibilities.

as a Muppet elephant's eye, the music rose to crescendo, and the *Sesame Street* cast began to sing the title song: *O . . . !*

And it pretty much ended there, because *Sesame Street* was brought to you that day by the letter *O*. *Sesame Street* was brought to you by the letter *K* the next day, *L* on Wednesday, and . . . well, it took several weeks to complete the title song.

Thus I learned in this absolutely fabricated story[71] how to spell *Oklahoma!* OK! (And there's a reason why the musical was not set in Mississippi.)

I've learned many other things grammatical and orthographical from American musicals. For instance, how to pronounce *potato* (long *A*) vs. *potahto* (short *A*), in "Let's Call the Whole Thing Off," a George and Ira Gershwin song from a Fred Astaire/Ginger Rogers musical, *Shall We Dance.* (The song goes on to detail other variant pronunciations, like *neether/nyther, vanilla/vanella,* and *pajamas/p'jahmas.*) Critical information.

But, I contend mischievously and with avowed silliness, that despite hit Broadway runs, Hollywood musicals, and Broadway revivals, one of the musicals has been lying to us: *Grease* is *not* the word, the word, the word. "It's got groove, it's got meaning," goes the lyric. Since I don't know what the lyricist means by *groove*, I fail to grasp the meaning. Unless . . .

Unless we turn to other languages. (How's that for a transition?) Kate Burridge in *Blooming English* discusses one danger of using foreign words and phrases, especially in speech. She calls this danger "hyper-foreignization" and uses the French *coup de grace* ("blow of mercy") as an example. Most of us English types (guilty as charged) would pronounce this as "coo-day-gra," while the final

---

[71] It's a lie! A lie, I tell you!

syllable should actually be pronounced "gras." Burridge writes, "if you say 'gra' not 'gras' then you're actually pronouncing the French word for grease—so the blow of mercy becomes the blow of grease." And not the groove of grease?

What's more, when turning to other languages and understanding that so much of our vocabulary and vocabulary-building tools (such as prefixes and suffixes) comes from the classical languages, we clearly see that Greece, and not *Grease*, is the word, is the word, is the word.

STEINBECK, JOHN

File under "Toby, or Not Toby": The dog did not eat your homework.

OK, OK, it's a stretch to include this entry in a book of English misconceptions, but cut me some slack by assuming that the above-mentioned dog did not eat your *English* homework.

The classic "My dog ate my homework" excuse has actually worked in the real world but twice. Once was when you were late for your book report about Steinbeck's novelette *Of Mice and Men*. The other was when you *wrote* the novelette *Of Mice and Men,* and I'm talking about *you,* Mr. Steinbeck.

John Steinbeck's first title for that particular classic was *Something That Happened.* Little did Steinbeck know. You see, there is a tale that Steinbeck's dog ate his (Steinbeck's, not the dog's) manuscript of *Of Mice and Men* before he was to have submitted it to his editor. The tale is probably only partially right. Toby—*not* mouse and man's best friend, I dare say—was the pet that tore apart Steinbeck's manuscript in what might be the most prominent example of what happens when a dog chases and catches its tale. Whether actual eating of Steinbeck's words was involved depends on how literally you take Steinbeck's post-destruction comments. "Two months' work to do over," Steinbeck wrote. "There was no other draft. I was pretty mad, but the poor little fellow may have been acting critically. I didn't want to ruin a good dog for a manuscript I'm not sure is good at all. . . . I'm not sure [that] Toby didn't know what he was doing when he ate the first draft. I have promoted Toby-dog to be lieutenant-colonel in charge of literature."

The main point of astonishment in this tale isn't in canine literary tastes. It lies in the fact that Steinbeck rewrote *Of Mice and Men* **IN TWO MONTHS** (all emphasis intended). It took me longer to write this entry.

Now, remember that the book's eventual title was inspired by lines in the Robert Burns poem "To a Mouse": "The best laid schemes o' mice an' men/ gang aft agley."

In this case, "The best laid schemes o' Stein an' Beck, gags arfed To-by," indeed.

WORD (NEGATED)
English has no words at all.

Or so has been claimed. I turn the lectern over to Dr Goodword, who at alphadictionary.com writes:

> No one has ever been able to define the word "word" despite gargantuan efforts to do so. The linguistic concept of word: an analytic bibliography by Alphonse

Juilland and Alexandra Roceric is a 118-page bibliography of books and articles (unsuccessfully) attempting
to define "word" over the past 3 millennia. Why can no
one define "word"? Maybe because words simply do not
exist; rather, the sentences we speak are composed of
lexemes and morphemes and these two linguistic
objects differ too much to be subsumed under
one concept.

Well, then.

I might tend to disagree that words do not exist, as I suspect
I've used a few in my life (including this very day!), just as I've
eaten lasagna a time or two. There's no non sequitur involved in
those two claims, because Dr Goodword's argumentation sounds
to me like arguing that lasagna simply doesn't exist because the
dish we eat is composed of pasta and meat sauce, and these two
nutritional objects differ too much to be subsumed under one
concept. Still, eating the nonexistent pasta seems to be making
me fatter. And as for you, kind reader, likely thinner than I am, I
can not say with complete confidence that you are eating lasagna
as you read this, but I'm absolutely confident that you are reading
something, those little units I'll take comfort in continuing to
refer to as words.

The crux of Dr Goodword's argument is that a lexeme is a verb,
a noun, an adjective—all of which connote objects, actions, and
concepts (apparently all concepts other than the concept of a
linguistic unit unifying morphemes and lexemes to communicate
a specific meaning) in the real world. A morpheme is a cognitive
view of the lexeme, expressed with prefixes and suffixes. *Quick* is a
lexeme. *-ly* is a morpheme. *Quickly* is . . . well, what it is.

Why can't the tandem work of these two -*emes* be considered a unified, well-meshed "word"? Notes the good Dr: "Current evidence now suggests that the two processes [envisioning a lexeme and conceptualizing how the morpheme acts or is acted upon] take place in two different parts of the brain." And the two processes of cooking lasagna [boiling pasta and baking it in the meat sauce] take place in two different parts of the kitchen.

So, because lasagna doesn't exist, I believe I'll have another helping.

The Few-Chore! (which of course is how we'll be spelling *future* in the future)

So what does the future of English hold? Change, confusion, arguments, dilettantes of the dictionary fuming and kneejerking, Swiftian dictates to embalm the language and Shavian efforts to streamline it. It's perhaps odd to evoke such figures of the past to invoke and perhaps provoke the future, but with all due respect to the antiplatitudinous, everything old is new again.

Various projections have been made about whither goes the language (and whether it will wither), ranging from the deteriorating distinction between using singular and plural verbs to loss of *whom* entirely,[72] to failed attempts at kompleet fonetik speling overhawl (*thru! nite!*) engaging in raged battles with failed attempts to preferveft þe marvelous Englisc Tonge (*through! night!*), we thankest þee (and the fact that my cute archaisms here are garbled at best is further proof of how futile both efforts will be).

In the future we will see the loosening of rules, and the tightening of rules. We will see debate over change, and we will see change slip past us as we continue to worry about lightning rods like *hopefully* and *impact* and sentences that end with infinitives or splitting prepositions or whatever the hell the argument is about this week. And we will pass the new language, as in the title of a classic Moody Blues album, *To Our Childrens Childrens Children*—except the band used apostrophes, and I didn't on purpose, as you see as we peer into our "childrens" few-chore!:

CHILDREN
File under "Pluralizationses": In a thousand years, *childrenses* may not be an inappropriate plural.

---

[72] For which I say, don't let the door hit you in the assem, *whom*.

"You childrens go out and play!"

That's bad grammar in that made-up quote, right? Agreed. After all, why should you pluralize an already plural noun? We could say that it's proper to instead say, "You children go out and play!" But then I would again retort, why should you pluralize an already plural noun?

In Old English, the plural of *child* was *childer,* using -er as the indicator of plural. But in Middle English, speakers began adding the *-en* convention in the line of *brethren,* plural of *brother.* So, perhaps we could say that it's proper to instead say, "You childer go out and play!"

To which I would again retort, why should you pluralize an already plural noun? In older Old English, the plural of *child* was *child,* just as *deer* and *moose* are both singular and plural. "You child go out and play! That's the fourth time I've told you!"

So, because we've pluralized the pluralized version of the plural by jury-rigging the word *children,* why not keep the momentum further pluralizing to the form *childrens* . . . which, by the way is a documented plural of the word for young'ns (along with *childs, childe* and *childers* . . .). What's a mother to do?

HELL OH HELL

u r wrong if you think the dangers of Internetspeak lie only with such elocutions as *lol.*

A number of intriguing and sometimes troubling language trends are arising from the chitchatternet. On that topic, most people would immediately point to such threats as using *u r* instead of "you are," writing *ne* instead of any, of *lol* becoming a full word (which it is indeed threatening to do, spelled *lawl*, though I would have predicted the current spelling pronounced "el-oh-el"), and on and on and on. Troubling, yes, but for the most part these are emailisms, forumisms, chatroomisms, and often bloggisms. Forgive them? Tolerate them? No, but do keep in mind that we are seeing these days more verbal-communication-through-keyboard than we've ever seen.

For me, these oftentimes *Amateur Hour* initialisms and other bizarre "word" forms, despite their garishness, will have less ultimate deteriorative effect than a more subtle misuse I see condoned by the pros on beautifully designed, carefully constructed websites.

On many such websites, users login to a log-in page, when they should "log in." How do you create tenses of the verb *login*? I login, I loginned, I have loginned? How do you conjugate it? I login, you login, she logins (or worse yet, logsin)?[73]

Similarly, on many websites, users signup for email newsletters, and generally receive a confirmation of that signup, when they should instead "sign up" (verb) to receive the notification of signup (noun). Manuals instruct you to startup your computer rather than "start up" the machine, to backup files rather than "back up" files. Fillout some forms, while you're at it. Seems we're sucking out the spaces between verbs and adverbs, probably because some computer geeks believe we need to add extra space to the infinity of the Internet to make room for all the blogs out there.

And are such usages sneaking out into the rest of the world? Of course they are. Like an instruction I recently saw: "Turnover your badge." It must be smeared with icing.

Such misuses standout to me, prompting me to standup and speakout against them. Don't messup or screwup: As verbs, "log in," "sign up," "start up," "back up," "fill out," "stand up," "speak

---

[73] The inability to complete the conjugation technically makes this verb form more than just annoying. It makes it defective. In oh so many ways. See "*Can*" on page 165 for related ranting.

out," "mess/screw up," and others with similar construction are verb phrases of two words each, damnit! . . . oops.

EMOTICONS

File under "Icon, emot-": I am not the bearer of pleasant punctuational predictions.

You're all certainly familiar with the Internet e-babble convention of grouping punctuation to form pictures as if they were Asian pictograms or Egyptian hieroglyphics. Emoticons—those cute punctuation trains—have been around for a number of years. Here a few examples. For the Internet-challenged, tilt your head to the left to "read" the pictures:

:) *smiley face*

;-) *knowing wink*

:o *wide-mouthed surprise*

:O *even greater surprise, or maybe that's a pig*

#-) *wasted*

{8>(} *stuffy guy wearing glasses dissatisfied with his big pointy nose, bad toupée and scruffy chin whiskers, though of course I made that one up*

Now, the bad news, something that won't make you :) and probably will make you :o or :O and will certainly convince you that I'm #-)

What I'm about to suggest is blasphemy of blasphemies, but this is my fear, and this is my prediction: Some emoticons might find their way into everyday use in decades to come . . . to the point of becoming formal punctuation. That will be a long time away, yet remember that language's many evolutions include that of our punctuation. At one time, we had no punctuation marks at all—and today we use a variety of strokes and flyspecks and squiggles that weren't at all like the early punctuation marks. For a time, for instance, what we call a slash or virgule (/) was used the way commas are used today. (Also see "Comma Faults" on page 172 for more information.)

However, emoticons don't function as punctuation—*yet*. Some of these protocharacter combinations could very well crawl out of the sea, develop four legs, and eventually stand on two feet. I don't mean that we'll see any sort of sentence with a smiley face replacing ellipses, for instance, though the thought intrigues. We have at least two punctuation symbols that signal the sentence's intent, as opposed to most other symbols, which indicate such concepts as relationships (colons and hyphens, for example), isolation (like the parentheses that surround this phrase), and rhythms (including commas and periods, though their use is far more functional than just establishing rhythm). The two symbols indicating intent are the exclamation point, which helpfully allows us to see the difference between "I'm on fire" and "I'm on fire!," and the question mark, which signals not only interrogation but also doubt. *Doubt? How could that be?*—and thus my point.

These two inflectional symbols are often used together. *Together, you say?! That's absurd!* In 1962, an advertising exec named Martin K. Speckter suggested in a *TYPEtalks Magazine* article that the symbols be merged into one symbol, eventually called an interrobang (the "bang" being printer lingo for "exclamation point"). *What?! Merge them?!* Not exactly an unprecedented marriage, as evidenced by $, formed by wedding two characters, including the letter *S*. (We're not sure which specific letter was superimposed over the *S*, as there are several theories of the symbol's origin. However, we do know that Martin K. Speckter did *not* propose the symbol in *MONEYtalks Magazine*.)[74]

So, we find ourselves with already-established symbols that tell us how a sentence is spoken, or that signal the writer's intent. Doubt, questioning, fury, urgency, astonishment—so why not one that officially signals that all the preceding was a joke?

In other words, I'm not serious :)

I think :O

TEH

We may soon be longing for the return of the obsolete character "thorn" (see page 188).

You've seen teh (er, the) misspelling if you've spent more than ten minutes in an Internet chat room: bad typing, quickly done, transposing *E* and *H* in *the* to create *teh*. We brought it on ourselves, of course. Keyboard arrangement was designed to *slow you down* when typing and force you into unnatural finger movements. Not for torture's sake, though my eighth-grade typing teacher wasn't clear on that point.

Early typewriter designers laid out the keys for ease of common keystroke combinations. Typists became so skilled that they out-typed the typewriters, and the typebars flying up to smack letters onto the paper would jam up like coils of long-stored Christmas tree lights in the typing frenzy. The answer? Key

---

[74] And here, a speculative thought: Mewonders (kind of like *methinks*), if there's any connection between Mr. Speckter creating new punctuation and Ambrose Bierce's definition of the word *fly-speck*: "n. The prototype of punctuation. It is observed by Garvinus that the systems of punctuation in use by the various literary nations depended originally upon the social habits and general diet of the flies infesting the several countries. These creatures, which have always been distinguished for a neighborly and companionable familiarity with authors, liberally or niggardly embellish the manuscripts in process of growth under the pen, according to their bodily habit, bringing out the sense of the work by a species of interpretation superior to, and independent of, the writer's powers."

positioning that would lead to awkward reaching and such. No more frenzies. No more jamming. No more efficiency. And lots more *teh*. Now, in the age of computers, no more typebars. No electrons colliding and sparking when furious typing fingers have at. But yet, lots more *teh*.

Let me frighten you further. This transposition mistake is common enough, and even intentionally used enough in webspeak, that *the* is in danger of mutating, or, at the very least, spawning a new definite article with specific nuance, though I won't be speculating about what that nuance might be.

I hope you're not thinking about getting any sleep tonight.

R., U.

The development of Internet initial-speak is not exactly a shock.

"I wish you wd tell me how u.r. when u. write."

So reads a message I spotted on the Internet just the other day. Chat rooms and emails are filled with such elocutions: *lol* for "laugh out loud," *brb* for "be right back," *ic* for "I see," and *DIICFOWMETGMAFOMP* for "damn it, I can't figure out why my English teacher gave me an *F* on my paper." The initial-speak that astounds me most is *ne*, which is not what Monty Python knights say, but is instead the incredibly keystroke-saving letter combination *n-e*, phonetic for "any."

Which brings us back to the illiterate soul who wrote "wd" for "would" and "u.r." for "you are." That would be, specifically, the illiterate Thomas Hardy—author of *Far from the Madding Crowd, Jude the Obscure,* and *Tess of the d'Urbervilles*—in an 1862 letter. I did indeed spot it on the Internet—in an *Oxford English Dictionary* online citation.

OW. EOINA.[75]

---

[75] Oh well. Everything old is new again.

Final Words

Infamous last words, hoping to become famous.

THE SECTION ABOUT "FINAL WORDS," NOT SO FINAL BECAUSE IT'S PART I

The word *word* is not the twenty-ninth most-used word in the English language.

Yet. According to *The Reading Teachers Book of Lists, Third Edition,* the word *word* is the thirtieth most-used word in English, and as a supporter of the word *word,* I keep pointing out that the thirtieth most-used word in English is the word *word,* hoping to elevate it to at least twenty-ninth in the fourth edition. I'll keep you posted.

THE SECTION ABOUT "FINAL WORDS," WHICH (WE ALL HOPE) MIGHT TRULY BE FINAL BECAUSE IT'S PART II

I'm obviously not done yet.

Despite all the changes in English over the centuries—the respellings, the intensifications, the redefinings, and the confusions; the consonant shift upheavals and the continental drifts; the invasions and surrenders; the neologisms and crumbling antiquities; the poetic, the didactic, the ephemeral, the persnickitorial—despite all this swirl and vortex and shimmering change, there is one constant. I find comfort and invigoration in a word that we continue to spell just as we did in Old English, a word that has seen variant spellings over the centuries, yet today retains the spelling just as the author of *Beowulf* used it. You'll see its familiar face in this excerpt from *Beowulf:*

> *Him se yldesta ondswarode,*
> *werodes wisa, word-hord onleac:*
> *"We synt gumcynnes Geata leode*
> *ond Higelaces heorðgeneatas."*

> *To him the stateliest spake in answer;*
> *the warriors' leader his word-hoard unlocked:—*
> *"We are by kin of the clan of Geats,*
> *and Hygelac's own hearth-fellows we."*

The word, of course, is *word.*

And from mine own word-hoard: So much that you know about English is wrong. So much much more that you know about English is exquisitely, vibrantly, resonantly right. Sing our modern songs of *Beowulf,* my friends. Sing them in quiet conversations and in chat rooms and talking in your sleep. Sing them in poetry and novels and postcards. Sing me thy words, my kind hearth-fellows, sing me the centuries.

Afterword

On these pages, I've presented a few smartass mock etymologies and rules (and of course, I've identified them as just that). And I've neologized a number of words (with, I admit, unabashed glee). I'm the first to suppose that someone will pick up those facetious and sarcastic falsities out of context, deliberately or otherwise, and circulate them as truth. This does not bother me. First, because it may be the first time that anyone has adopted my "conclusions" as the truth, and second because I spent some time as a youth on a farm, and I realize the importance of reseeding the field, and of planting the falsities that I will harvest in further volumes.

I'm just kidding about that. I think.

Better yet, email me your favorite falsities, stupid notions, persnickitations, and bullshitternetisms about our glorious English language to Bill@EverythingYouKnowAboutEnglishIsWrong.com (or at Bill@WhyTheHellCan'tYouGetaShorterWebsiteNameForYourBook. whew!), and I'll attempt to persuade my brilliant and perceptive publisher to throw money at me while I vigilantly discount submitted delusions in sequels to this book. Until that happens, however, I concede that there's great poetry in the English phrase that has been with us for many centuries, "Would you like fries with that?"

Selected Bibliography

AN UNBIBLIOGRAPHIC BIBLIOGRAPHY
Ogden Nash did not write this poem.

Shake and shake
the catsup bottle
first none'll come
and then a lot'll

That's Richard Armour, though it has been wrongly attributed to Nash. To Mr. Armour, a word of thanks.

Which is already inaccurate, because I've used several words to this point.

And that's the kind of joke that Richard Armour made in his delightful, learned romps like *The Classics Reclassified, It All Started with Columbus,* and *American Lit Relit.* Look him up. His writings may come from the days before squeeze ketchup bottles, but they will live far longer than the bio-undegradeable plastic in those bottles.

And that's my point in this bibliography.

Relax, enjoy. We argue so damn much over this language. Let's instead celebrate it.

Start with Armour. Then go find Dave Barry's "Mr. Language Person" columns ("brought to you this week by Ray's House of Fine

Adverbs. Remember Ray's motto: 'Proudly Serving You, Eventually'").
Absolutely do not ignore Steven Pinker's *The Language Instinct*. Check
out Willard Espy's *Almanac of Words at Play* and Richard Lederer's
energetic *Anguished English* and its many followups. Absorb yourself
in David Crystal's numerous linguistic travelogues. And for overall
good and informed reading about the history of English, I can't recommend the first book on my unbibliography enough:

BOOKS
- *Our Marvelous Native Tongue,* by Robert Claiborne, Three Rivers
  Press (1987).
- *The Language Instinct: How the Mind Creates Language,* Steven
  Pinker, William Morrow and Co., New York (1994).
- *The Fight for English: How Language Pundits Ate, Shot and Left,* by
  David Crystal, Oxford University Press, Oxford/New York (2006).
- *The Dictionary of Disagreeable English: A Curmudgeon's
  Compendium of Excruciatingly Correct Grammar,* by Robert
  Hartwell Fiske, Writer's Digest Books, Cincinnati (Deluxe Edition
  2006).
- *Devious Derivations: Popular Misconceptions and More Than 1,000
  True Origins of Common Words and Phrases,* by Hugh Rawson,
  Crown Publishers, New York (1994).
- *Word Myths: Debunking Linguistic Urban Legends,* by David Wilton,
  Oxford University Press, Oxford/New York (2004).
- *Grammatically Correct: The Writer's Essential Guide to Punctuation,
  Spelling, Style, Usage and Grammar,* by Anne Stilman, Writer's
  Digest Books, Cincinnati (2004).
- *Ballyhoo, Buckaroo, and Spuds: Ingenious Tales of Words and Their
  Origins,* by Michael Quinion, Smithsonian Books, Washington
  D.C. (2004).

- *The Barnhart Concise Dictionary of Etymology,* ed. by Robert K. Barnhart, HarperCollinsPublishers, New York (1995).
- *The New Shorter Oxford English Dictionary on Historical Principles,* vols I and II, ed. by Lesley Brown, Clarendon Press, Oxford (1993).
- *A Browser's Dictionary and Native's Guide to the Unknown American Language,* by John Ciardi, Harper & Row, New York (1980), and *A Second Browser's Dictionary and Native's Guide to the Unknown American Language,* by John Ciardi, Harper & Row, New York (1983).
- *A History of English in Its Own Words,* by Craig M. Carver, HarperCollins, New York (1991).
- *Merriam-Webster New Book of Word Histories,* ed. by Frederick C. Mish, Merriam-Webster, Springfield MA (1991).
- *Morris Dictionary of Word and Phrase Origins,* 2nd ed., by William and Mary Morris, Harper & Row, New York (1988).

WEBSITES

- oed.com, the *Oxford English Dictionary* online
- wordorigins.org, from David Wilton and a lively discussion forum
- worldwidewords.org, Michael Quinion's website
- bartleby.com, which includes The *American Heritage Dictionary of the English Language*
- word-detective.com, operated by Evan Morris
- dictionary.com and the related thesaurus.com
- etymonline.com
- funwords.com, Martha Barnette's website
- The Maven's Word of the Day, http://www.randomhouse.com/wotd/index.pperl?action=dly__alph_arc&fn=word
- verbivore.com, Richard Lederer's website

Index of Things You Don't Know

(words, phrases and letters)

(page numbers in boldface italic indicate entries where
the indexed item is a primary subject)

Index of Things You Don't Know

(concepts, subjects and nonsense)

(page numbers in boldface italic indicate entries where
the indexed item is a primary subject)

About the Author

Bill Brohaugh is the former editor of *Writer's Digest* magazine and the former editorial director of Writer's Digest Books. He is the author of *Unfortunate English* and *Professional Etiquette for Writers*, and is the director of *English through the Ages*.